HAWKING

HAWKING

Written by
JIM OTTAVIANI

Art by
LELAND MYRICK

Coloring by
AARON POLK

First Second
NEW YORK

First Second

Published by First Second
First Second is an imprint of Roaring Brook Press,
a division of Holtzbrinck Publishing Holdings Limited Partnership
120 Broadway, New York, NY 10271
firstsecondbooks.com

This biography, while unauthorized, was compiled with
the knowledge and cooperation of its subject.

Library of Congress Control Number: 2018944919

Our books may be purchased in bulk for promotional, educational, or business use.
Please contact your local bookseller or the Macmillan Corporate and Premium Sales Department at
(800) 221-7945 ext. 5442 or by email at MacmillanSpecialMarkets@macmillan.com.

FIRST
EDITION

First paperback edition, 2021
Edited by Calista Brill and Casey Gonzalez
Cover design by Andrew Arnold
Interior book design by Rob Steen and Molly Johanson
Color by Aaron Polk

Printed in China by 1010 Printing International Limited, North Point, Hong Kong

Drawn and inked with Sakura Pigma Micron pens on Canson Pro Layout Marker paper. Colored digitally in Photoshop

ISBN 9-781-250-77794-2 (paperback)
1 3 5 7 9 10 8 6 4 2

Don't miss your next favorite book from First Second! For the latest updates
go to firstsecondnewsletter.com and sign up for our enewsletter.

BY ART
WE LIVE

For Kat and Leland, wonderful traveling companions
——J.O.

For Andrea, who helped me find the path
——L.M.

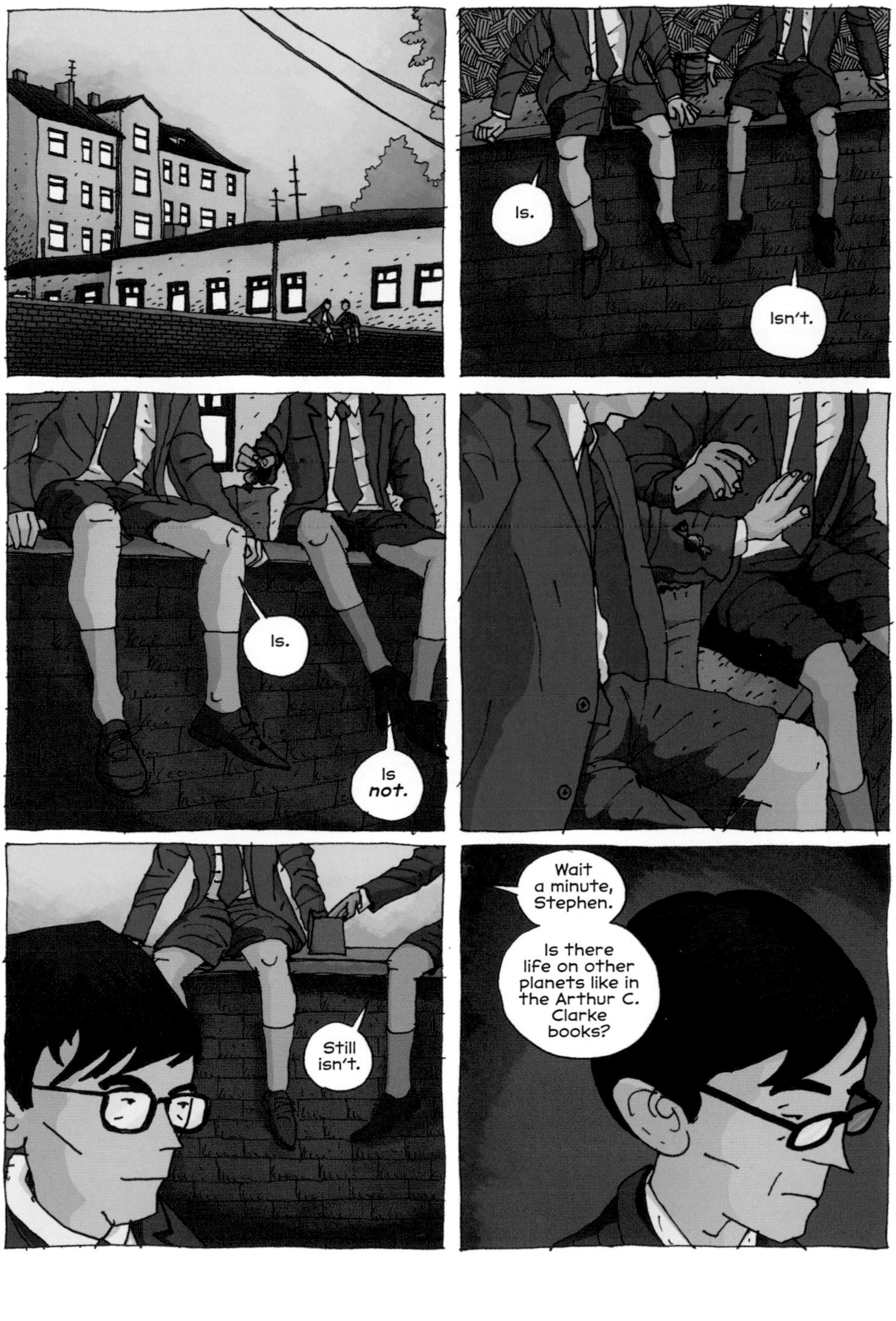
Is.
Isn't.
Is.
Is not.
Still isn't.
Wait a minute, Stephen.
Is there life on other planets like in the Arthur C. Clarke books?

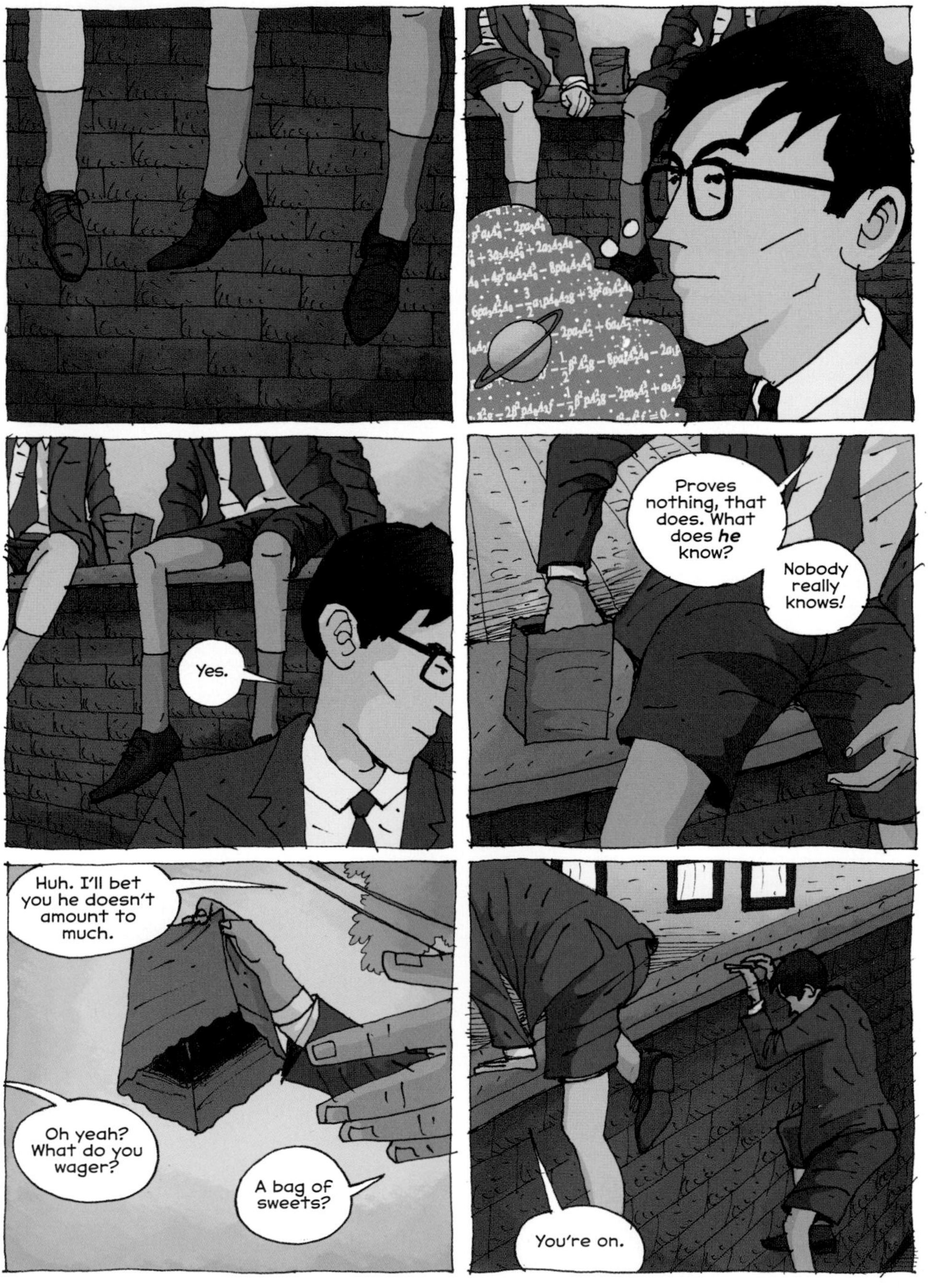
Yes.
Proves nothing, that does. What does *he* know?
Nobody really knows!
Huh. I'll bet you he doesn't amount to much.
Oh yeah? What do you wager?
A bag of sweets?
You're on.

I DON'T KNOW WHO COLLECTED ON THAT BET.

HAWKING

Three hundred years after Galileo died (January 1942)

Twelve years earlier...

OXFORD

You're in line for...?

They say this shop has some bread.

Ah. Thank you.

They'll feed me well in the hospital, after all, so...

And after, I'll still be on extra rations, at least for a while.

But evenings might drag until...

Are you all right, ma'am?

Yes, I'm... I'm fine, but thank you very much for asking. Just waiting for someone to arrive.

And deciding how to pass the time.

DING

DING

I was born on
January 8, 1942.

Exactly 300 years after Galileo died.

After the war we lived in Highgate, North London, until 1950, then moved to St. Albans.

By then I had two sisters, Mary and Philippa.

I remember some things about our house quite distinctly.

14 HILLSIDE ROAD, ST. ALBANS

It was a large Victorian about twenty miles north of London.

I'll show you my room.

What room, what room? Who said it was yours?

Sarah said this one should be mine.

Well, I suppose that's all right, then.

A favorite cousin of ours had recommended I choose the room that had probably been a maid's at one time.

Part of its appeal was that I could escape by climbing onto the roof of the bicycle shed.

I eventually discovered 11 ways out of the house.

Mary only ever guessed ten of them.

That took a number of years, though, and even then my friends entered in the usual way.

Hi, Basil. Come on up.

The house was big, formerly elegant, and not in good repair.

After fixing what was essential to move in, my father didn't do much more than patch things up from then on. He wasn't very adept at such things.

Africa.

Hand me that, Basil, wouldn't you, please?

And he wasn't home 75% of the time anyway. He was a medical researcher studying tropical diseases, on location.

Are you going to study medicine?

I suppose he wants me to, but...

I prefer chemistry. Or physics.

Not sure.

Didn't expect *that!*

Chemistry is definitely more fun.

Stephen?!

Everything's fine, Mother. Just doing a bit of an experiment.

Well... all right. But it's dinnertime. Would Basil like to stay?

Yes.

You'd like to stay, wouldn't you?

Sure.

Nonono, Monopoly isn't adaptable enough. I've an idea for a much more interesting game. I'll show you the detailed outline after we eat, but here's the gist: You start with...

Hawkingese (1954)

...barely a word from anyone else, even to pass the food!

Who can understand that lot, anyway? They all speak almost as fast as Stephen.

So what *did* you talk about?

There's this game he's created called "dynasty." I can't figure it out, and I don't think he has it figured out either.

But as far as I can tell, playing will take forever, and I can't see how there's any way to *win*.

No way to win. That's our bet, mate!

Hah. We'll see.

Hallo, Church.

JOHN   BASIL   MICHAEL

King, McClenahan. What are you doing?

Walking to school. What are you doing?

Right. So clever.

ST ALBANS

Okay, yeah. I was telling John about dinner the other day. Over at Hawking's house.

Was everybody reading? It's *madness*. Nobody talking to anybody else.

13

Oh-ho. You want to talk to Mary, then? I'll let her know!

No. But sometimes I think it'd be easier than talking with her brother... Einstein.

You remember that time at school, while you lot were building your computing machine?

EXIT

Logical Unified... Universal...

Logical Uniselector Computing Engine. Just call it LUCE.

Speaking of logic, why don't you hold forth for us while we work, Michael?

We'd all like to hear more about those philosophical things you told me about before.

Right. Glad to.

Hey. Don't let him...

I was starting to get interested in the question of what kind of universe we live in. Was there a beginning?

Did that beginning require a God?

So while I liked chemistry for the explosions, I really was more interested in mathematics and physics. Physics was rather boring, though—too obvious.

It helped a little that I had an inspiring math teacher, Mr. Tahta.

Really. Go on, go on.

14

Is God bound by the laws of physics? (1958)

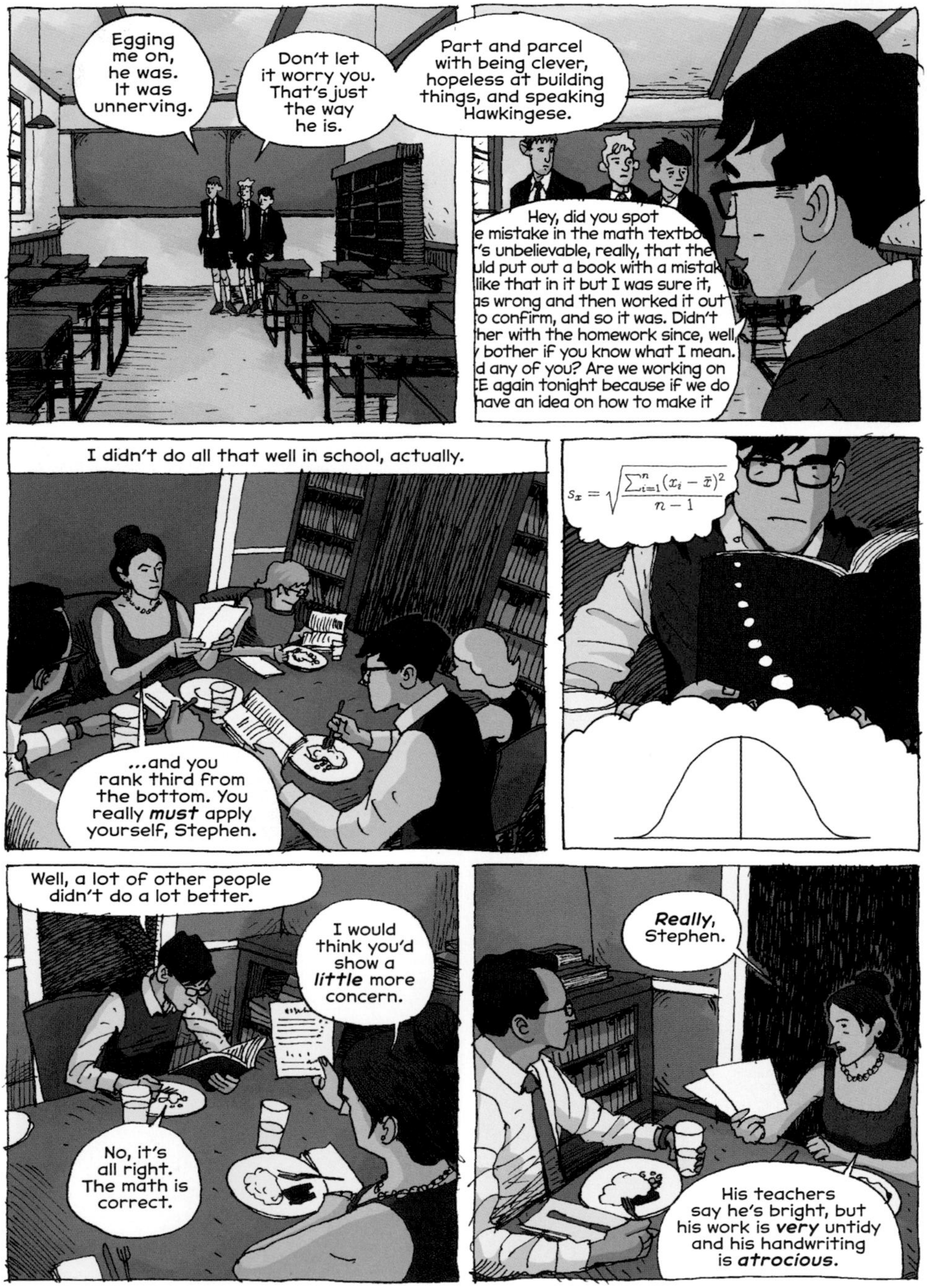
Egging me on, he was. It was unnerving.
Don't let it worry you. That's just the way he is.
Part and parcel with being clever, hopeless at building things, and speaking Hawkingese.
Hey, did you spot
e mistake in the math textbo
's unbelievable, really, that the
uld put out a book with a mistak
like that in it but I was sure it,
as wrong and then worked it out
o confirm, and so it was. Didn't
her with the homework since, well,
bother if you know what I mean.
d any of you? Are we working on
E again tonight because if we do
have an idea on how to make it
I didn't do all that well in school, actually.
...and you rank third from the bottom. You really *must* apply yourself, Stephen.
$s_x = \sqrt{\frac{\sum_{i=1}^{n}(x_i - \bar{x})^2}{n-1}}$
Well, a lot of other people didn't do a lot better.
I would think you'd show a *little* more concern.
No, it's all right. The math is correct.
Really, Stephen.
His teachers say he's bright, but his work is *very* untidy and his handwriting is *atrocious*.

In addition to school, we did the usual family things. Vacations...

(Until the county council forced my father to remove the caravan he'd bought.)

Are you sure you wouldn't like to join Philippa and me at the Victoria and Albert, or Mary at the Natural History Museum?

Culture...

SCIENCE MUSEUM

... Never mind.

Socializing...

Remember you're taking us to the dance this afternoon.

Yes, I remember. I look forward to it, in fact.

You're coming as well?

It's a dance, isn't it?

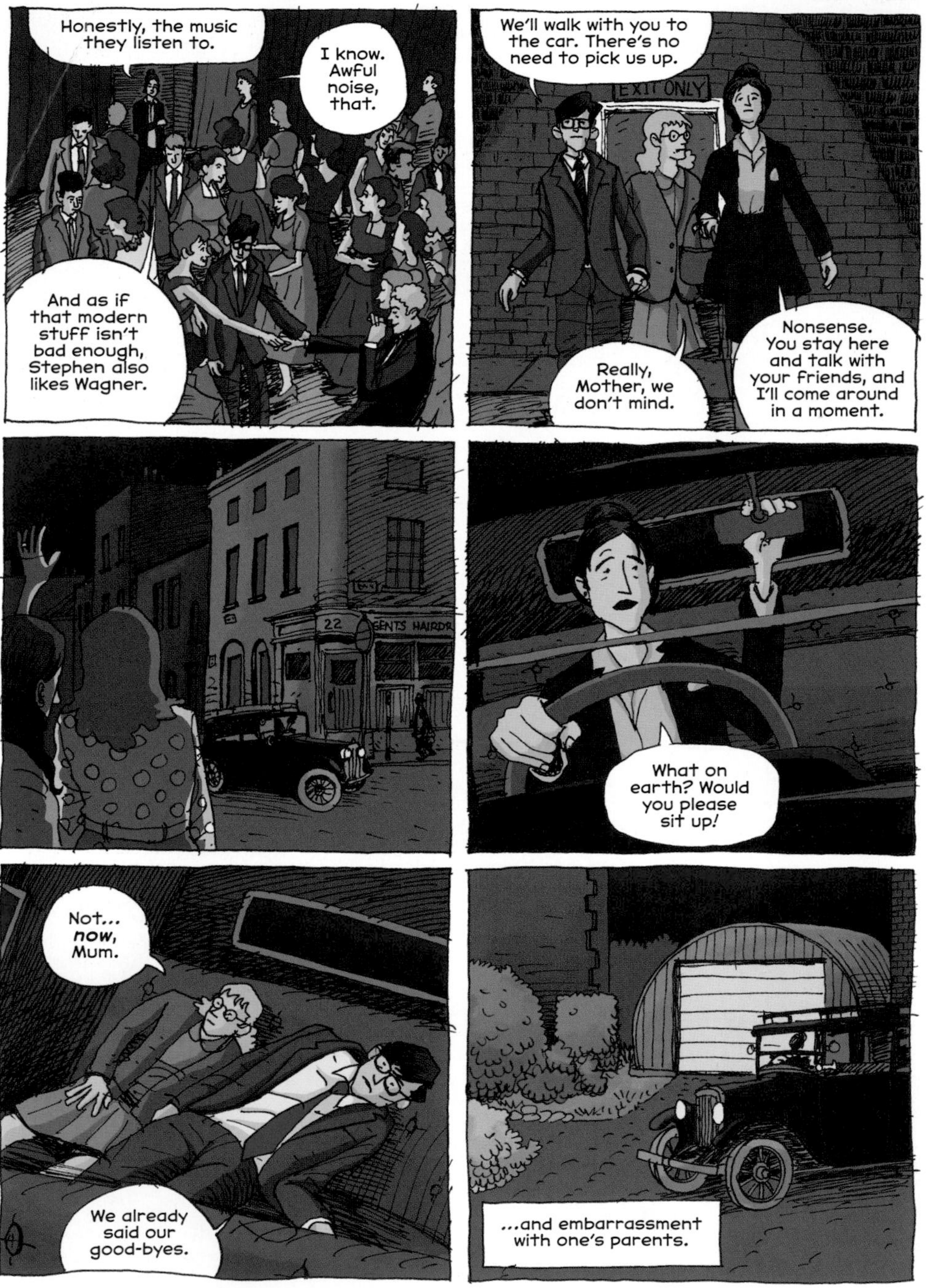
Honestly, the music they listen to.
I know. Awful noise, that.
And as if that modern stuff isn't bad enough, Stephen also likes Wagner.
We'll walk with you to the car. There's no need to pick us up.
EXIT ONLY
Really, Mother, we don't mind.
Nonsense. You stay here and talk with your friends, and I'll come around in a moment.
22
GENTS HAIRDR
What on earth? Would you please sit up!
Not... *now*, Mum.
We already said our good-byes.
...and embarrassment with one's parents.

Disappointing them too, I suppose.

But...

Yes, we know what you think about biology, but it's not as though your marks are so distinguished that you can be choosy.

No buts. People always need doctors. So, medicine. Physics or mathematics? Not a career.

One must keep one's options open, yes? And you like chemistry, so that's a good compromise, isn't it?

I shall be writing to University College in Oxford on your behalf.

In the end, I became a professor of mathematics...

...though it turns out that I didn't make any formal study of math after public school.

My family was in India much of my last year at St Albans. I stayed behind to study for A-level and university examinations.

I went up to Oxford for scholarship exams in March 1959.

Two days, five papers.

Interviews, both general and specialist, one with a panel of questioners.

Would you please repeat that, Mr. Hawking, and perhaps a bit more slowly?

Y-yes, of course.

19

I didn't think I had done very well.

I was wrong.

"The master, A. S. Goodhart, tells me that I was 'elected to an Open Scholarship in Natural Science at this College.'"

"'The maximum value of this Scholarship is £100 a year and I shall shortly be sending your father a form on which to apply for the discretionary emoluments attached to this award.'"

"I'll bring the form when I come to India."

"Etc., etc., and he's 'glad that you are coming to your father's College and hope you will enjoy your association with Univ.'"

"I will see you all soon."

"Love, Stephen."

"p.s. Tell Mary to say hello to all the camels and all the Dr. Mukerjis for me. And to please keep the Indian scale flute she bought tucked away…"

"She's right—
I will hate it."

I liked the
food there,
though.

When I returned to
England, I entered
Oxford.

I was 17.

I did not apply
myself.

...regardless, you can look up the proof in the
text. It's rather subtle, so for now you can
take the theorem as given.

And have
a look at the
following chapter
for next week.

Hawking?

...

Yes?

"About 1,000 hours' work in the three years..." (1959–1962)

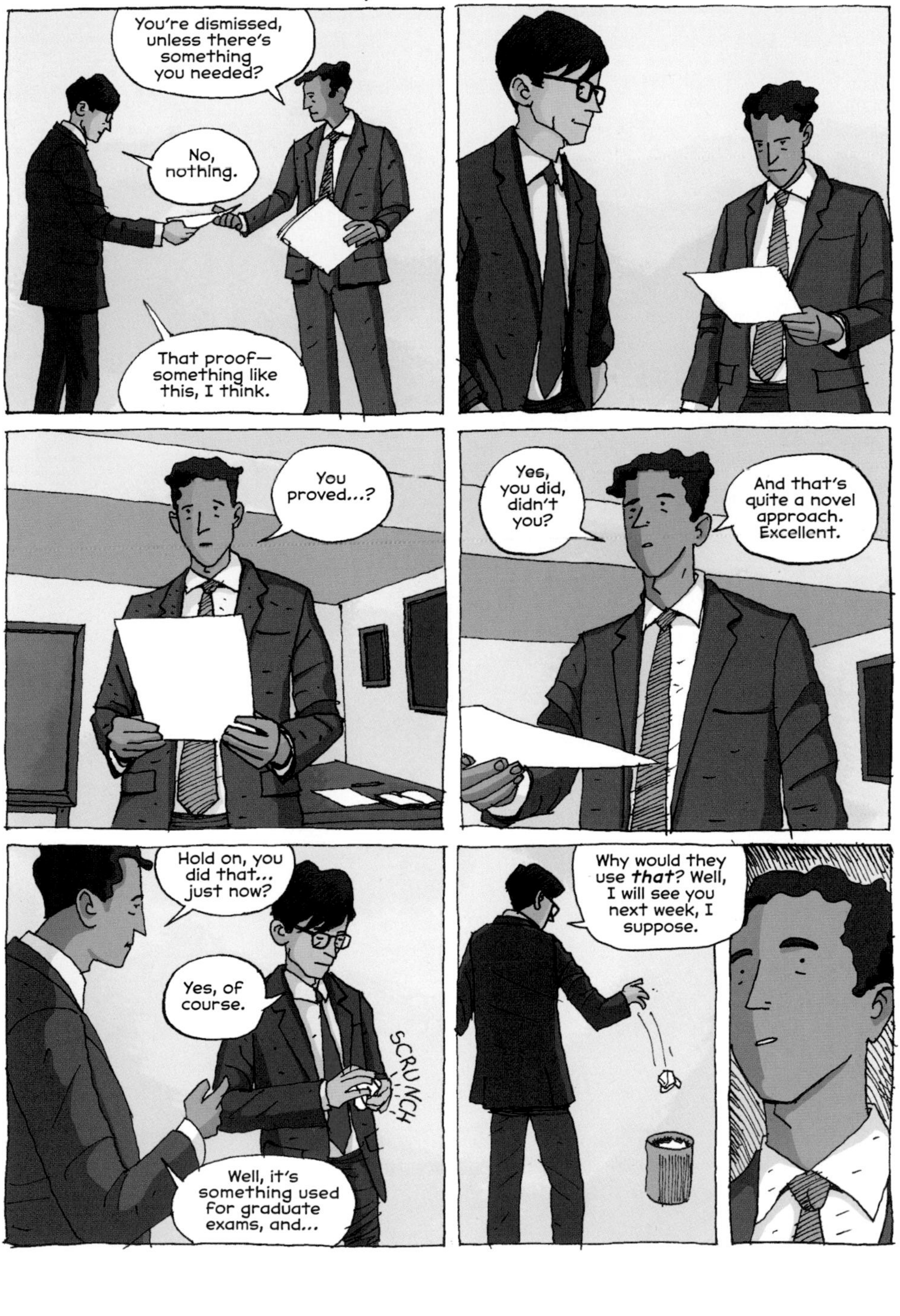
You're dismissed, unless there's something you needed?
No, nothing.
That proof—something like this, I think.
You proved...?
Yes, you did, didn't you?
And that's quite a novel approach. Excellent.
Hold on, you did that... just now?
Yes, of course.
SCRUNCH
Well, it's something used for graduate exams, and...
Why would they use *that*? Well, I will see you next week, I suppose.

Only "grey men" applied themselves, you see.

Hard workers.

Dull.

GORDON

RICHARD

DEREK

Steve. Come with us to the pub?

Sorry. Can't until next year.

Not my sort.

Derek, Gordon, and Richard were the only other physics students in my year.

Hard workers, actually, but not grey men.

We stuck together.

...more than that! Galileo did three important things, besides dropping objects off the leaning tower of Pisa.

And dying exactly 300 years...

...before you were born. We *know*, Steve.

As I was saying, with his telescope, he discovers the moons of Jupiter.

Everybody knows that.

Stuffy in here.

Right, and doing so confirmed that the Earth's not the center of it all.

And at the same time, when he looks at Jupiter through a telescope, it gets *bigger...*

But stars don't.

So, right, that tells him that stars are *much* farther away.

And when he sees more stars through the telescope than without it...

...he opens the door to there being more to the universe than we can see.

Or imagine.

That, plus basically giving us the scientific method...

Okay, okay. Fine. I'm convinced.

We didn't actually discuss history all that much, I don't think. But we got our grounding in classical physics à la Newton...

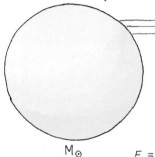

$M_\odot$

In other words, light as particles, equal and opposite forces defined as mass times acceleration, and calculus.

$$F_1 = F_2 = G \ \frac{M_\odot \times M_\oplus}{r^2}$$

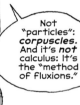

Not "particles": *corpuscles*. And it's *not* calculus: It's the "method of fluxions."

$M_\oplus$

$$\nabla \times \mathcal{H} = \mathcal{I}_e + \frac{\partial \mathcal{D}}{\partial t}$$

$$\nabla \times \mathcal{E} = -\mathcal{I}_m - \frac{\partial \mathcal{B}}{\partial t}$$

$$\nabla \cdot \mathcal{D} = \rho_e$$

$$\nabla \cdot \mathcal{B} = \rho_m$$

...And also electromagnetism per Maxwell and Faraday—light as waves, electricity and magnetism as two sides of the same coin.

...and have a go at the problems at the end of chapter 10 of Bleaney and Bleaney.

They're final honors questions, but attempt as many as you can.

Our second-year text *Electricity and Magnetism* was by a husband-and-wife team.

Thirteen of them. It's madness.

Derek, shall we put our heads together...

I'll come up to your room after lunch.

I'd like to try them on my own. Is that all right, Steve?

Of course.

...

Right, then.

We had a week.

I wasn't an early riser then. I still start my working day later than most, but for different reasons now.

The day they were due, though, the fellows rousted me out.

Early.

Come on. You have to eat breakfast now and again.

And we'll discuss where we've gotten to with the Bleaneys.

Well, I've managed one.

"I suppose I've only had time to do the first ten." (1961–1962)

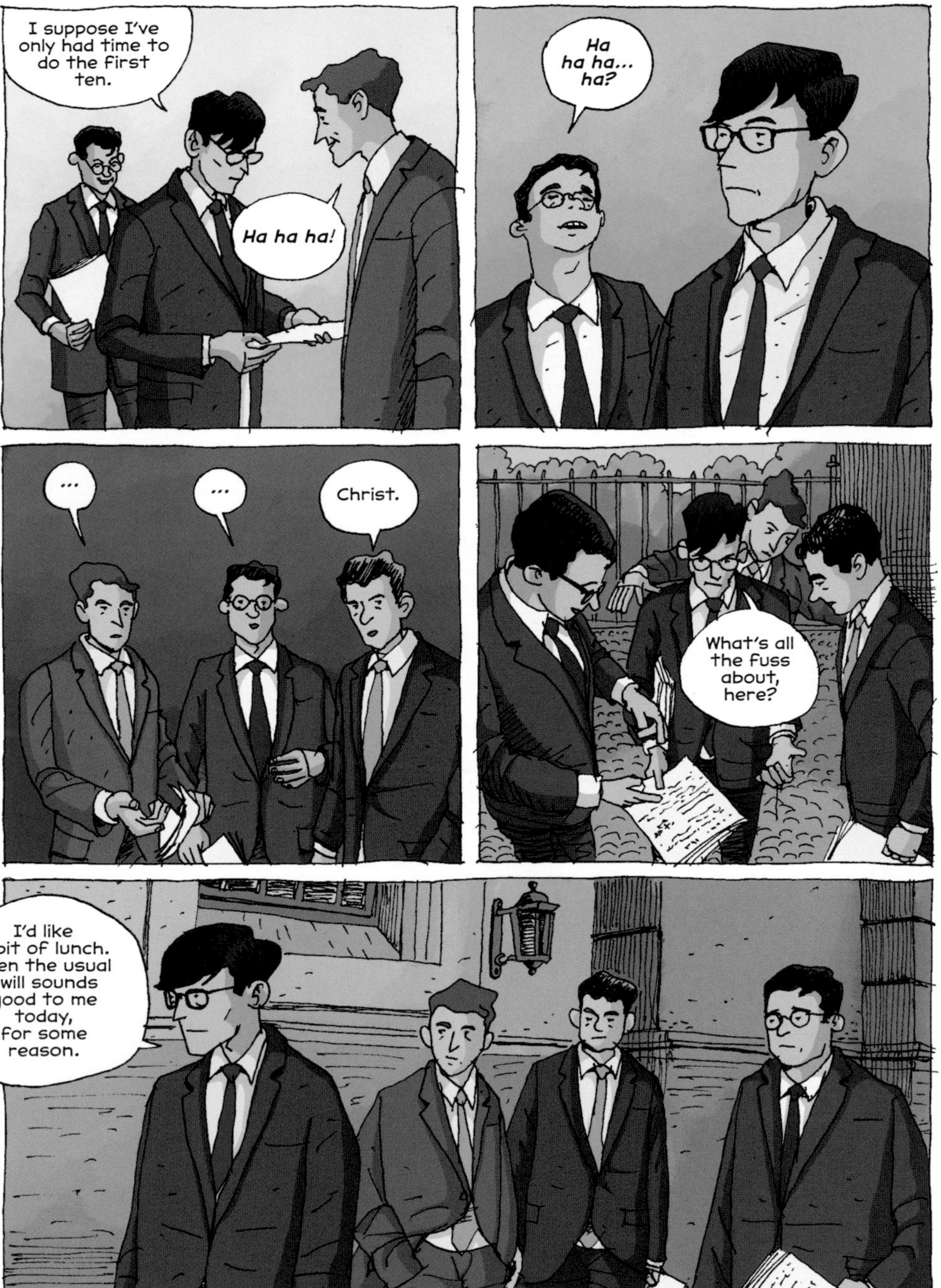
I suppose I've only had time to do the first ten.
Ha ha ha!
Ha ha ha... ha?
...
...
Christ.
What's all the fuss about, here?
I'd like a bit of lunch. Even the usual swill sounds good to me today, for some reason.

Gordon and I *did* work together in the laboratory portion of class.

I wasn't much of an experimentalist, though.

SPLORP!

So we kept data collection to a minimum...

Heh. Sorry. That's... enough, don't you think?

Oh, indeed.

...and did a *great* deal of analysis on what little we did collect.

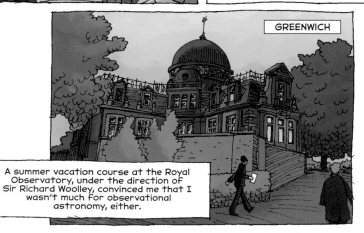

GREENWICH

A summer vacation course at the Royal Observatory, under the direction of Sir Richard Woolley, convinced me that I wasn't much for observational astronomy, either.

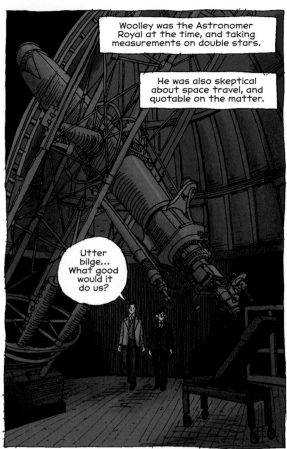

Woolley was the Astronomer Royal at the time, and taking measurements on double stars.

He was also skeptical about space travel, and quotable on the matter.

Utter bilge... What good would it do us?

This is how science gets done... It's one of the finest in the world, you know.

And tonight is particularly good for seeing. Have at it, lad!

Er.

It's not that there was anything I could damage there.

It's just...

Two hazy points of light, jumping around a bit?

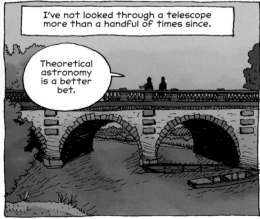

I've not looked through a telescope more than a handful of times since.

Theoretical astronomy is a better bet.

When my friends and I had arrived in Oxford, anybody who was anybody rowed, and never wore jeans.

THE ISIS (RIVER THAMES ABOVE IFFLEY LOCK)

Set ready!

I rowed from my second year on.

Well, others *rowed*. I was the cox.

Nicer clothes, and an opportunity to call the shots on the smart set.

Bow pair—
fall in.
Stern pair—
fall out.

I was excellent at it.

Sorry. Should've said holdwater, I s'pose.

I was loud, at least.

We still won a few races. And when we did, my crew were traditionalists when it came to rewarding the man at the rear.

In my third year I took a dive or two without any help.

Or so I'm told. I temporarily lost some memory after one, which worried my friends.

Who am I?

Steve Hawking. You're at Univ. You just fell down...

Right. C'n see that.

Nobody was *too* worried, though. They knew I'd always been clumsy, and eventually it all came back to me.

Who'm I?

I gave myself the Mensa test to make sure it *all* came back.

Which it did.

Mentally. So, no worries.

Betting on the grey men of Oxford (1962)

Oh, never mind.

Pointless things, neckties. Anyway, by the time I left, many things were changing.

The smart set never rowed, and jeans?

Now required.

I almost *didn't* leave, though.

Even though I studied as much as a few hours a day in the weeks leading up to final examinations, my years of... lack of work caught up with me.

I didn't do quite well enough to get a First—which I needed to go on to graduate study elsewhere.

I was right on the edge, so I requested an oral exam—a viva—as a tiebreaker.

I performed well. Particularly my closing statement...

If I get a First, I shall go to Cambridge. If I receive a Second, I'll remain here, at Oxford.

So I expect you will give me a First.

In 1962, I was off to Cambridge.

I wanted to get Fred Hoyle as an advisor for my research. He was quite famous.

And, as it turns out, too busy.

TRINITY HALL, CAMBRIDGE

He was also a bit of a celebrity, often quoted in newspapers, appearing on radio, and so on.

BBC

We now come to the question of applying observational tests to earlier theories of the expanding universe...

The advisor I got was Dennis Sciama. Not famous...

...but available. And a cosmologist.

SCIAMA

Stephen, is it? Come on in.

I had chosen cosmology over particle physics because the latter seemed too like botany at the time.

No, the bosons go over here...

There was no proper theory of the very small. Just lots of arranging things in families.

The very large, though? Einstein's general relativity was well established, and despite what Richard Feynman said after attending a conference on it...

Because there are *no experiments*, cosmology is not an active field, so few of the best men are working in it.

A brief history of relativity (1751–1962)

...well, the few best cosmologists were **very** good indeed.

Roger Penrose was at the conference Feynman complained about. He even introduced his diagrams there.

Roger and Sciama were good friends, so I soon learned of his work, and Penrose diagrams.

Infinity is represented by the sides of the square, and opposite sides are the same points in space.

And even if Feynman was correct, so what? A neglected field is ripe for development.

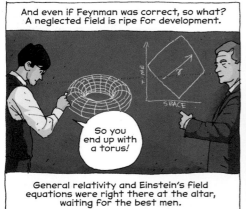

So you end up with a torus!

General relativity and Einstein's field equations were right there at the altar, waiting for the best men.

They'd been waiting a long time...

They'd also taken a long time to get there. Progress over the 100-plus years from Franklin's experiments to James Clerk Maxwell's theories was steady.

And Maxwell's theories were wildly successful— resulting in the age of electricity.

But Maxwell's theories treated light as a wave, and that was, if not a *problem*, at least a *puzzle*...

Because if it was a wave, it needed something to travel in.

Sound waves travel through air... ocean waves through water.

So for light waves, physicists postulated the *luminiferous aether*.

The puzzling thing about the aether was that even though it had to be everywhere—inside glass, permeating a perfect vacuum, etc....

...nobody could *detect* it.

The Earth's motion through it should create an aether wind blowing at us, for instance.

If light from Earth is heading upwind, it should slow down, and downwind, it should go faster.

Not an easy experiment to do, since as fast as the Earth moves around the Sun, light moves about 10,000 times faster.

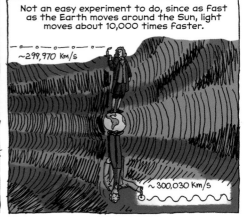

~299,970 km/s

~300,030 km/s

Michelson and Morley did manage this delicate measurement, though. The result?

Either the Earth drags the aether with it (unlikely), or there is no aether and light's a particle (more likely?), or...

...it moves at a constant speed either way. Which means light's different from other waves.

And everything else we know about. Really, really different.

And different—really, really different—from other particles, if it's a particle.

It is. And it's *corpuscle*, not *particle*.

Enter Einstein, and his explanation of the photoelectric effect.

It is okay, Sir Isaac. I will convince them about partic... corpuscles.

That's what he won his Nobel prize for, in fact. (Not relativity!)

Einstein figured out that light is composed of *photons*—discrete bundles of energy called "quanta."

And these photons can knock electrons—which physicists knew were particles that have a definite weight—around.

So light, which Maxwell had demonstrated *clearly* behaves like a wave, *clearly* behaves like it's made of particles!

I told you that in 1704. So what is all this talk of waves?

Light is a wave that behaves like a particle.

And it's a particle that behaves like a wave.

That crazy equivalency is a foundation of the Copenhagen interpretation—courtesy of Niels Bohr and Werner Heisenberg—of quantum theory, which embraces the apparent contradiction.

That's not what Einstein didn't like about the theory, but that's another story.

It's both, really. At the same time.

Well then, quantum theory is contradictory to every idea of reality that is reasonable, Niels.

Your idea of reality is too limited, old friend.

The important thing to remember is that in the realm of the very small—atoms, electrons, photons—things behave in *odd* ways.

And in 1905 Einstein started down a path toward identifying odd properties of the *very large* as well.

My friends called 1905 my *annus mirabilis.**

A Nobel prize-winning discovery and also special relativity and also...*the equation?* It's no exaggeration.

* "Extraordinary/miracle year"

42

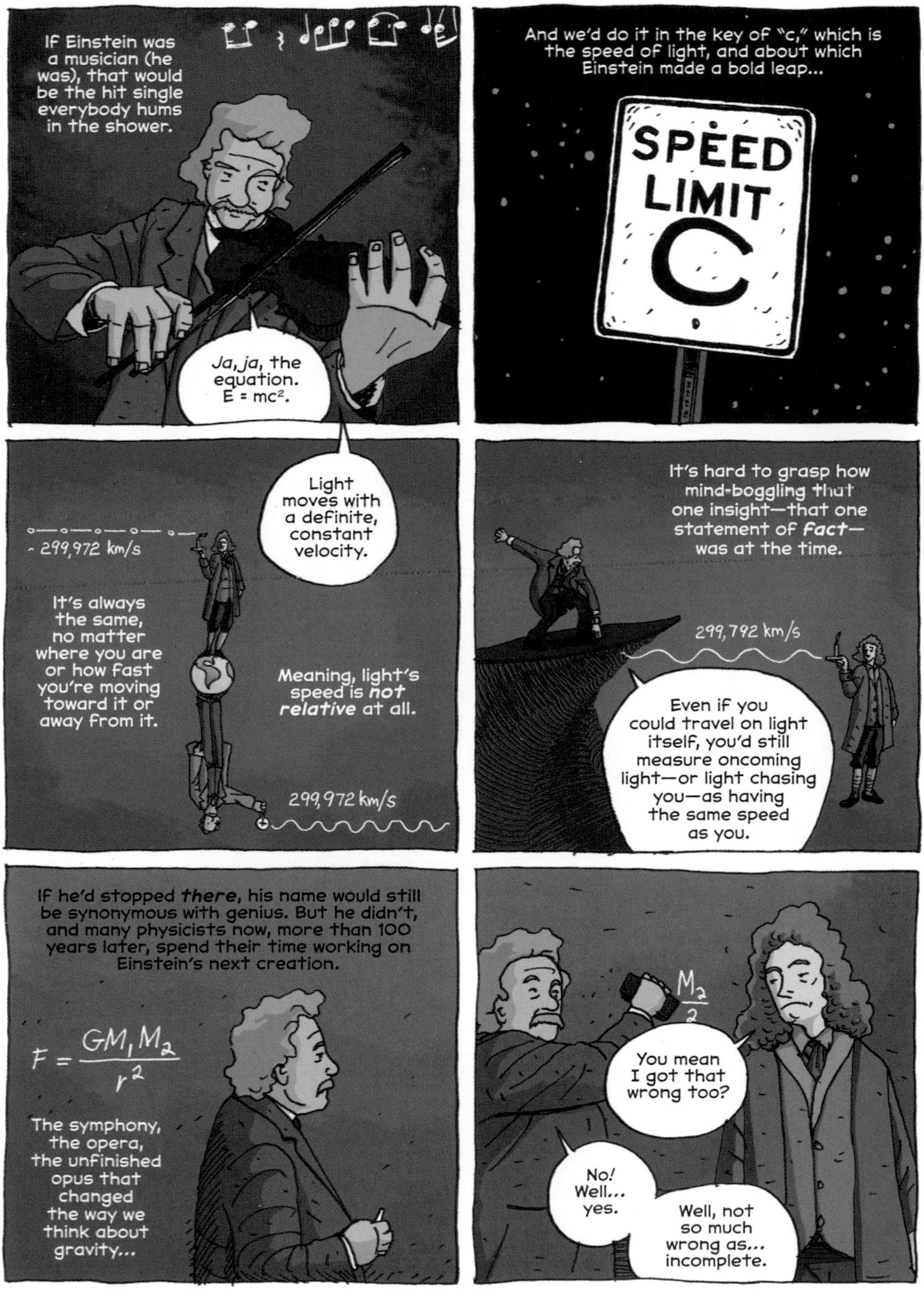
If Einstein was a musician (he was), that would be the hit single everybody hums in the shower.
Ja, ja, the equation. E = mc².
And we'd do it in the key of "c," which is the speed of light, and about which Einstein made a bold leap...
SPEED LIMIT C
Light moves with a definite, constant velocity.
299,972 km/s
It's always the same, no matter where you are or how fast you're moving toward it or away from it.
Meaning, light's speed is *not relative* at all.
299,972 km/s
It's hard to grasp how mind-boggling that one insight—that one statement of *fact*—was at the time.
299,792 km/s
Even if you could travel on light itself, you'd still measure oncoming light—or light chasing you—as having the same speed as you.
If he'd stopped *there*, his name would still be synonymous with genius. But he didn't, and many physicists now, more than 100 years later, spend their time working on Einstein's next creation.
$F = \frac{GM_1M_2}{r^2}$
The symphony, the opera, the unfinished opus that changed the way we think about gravity...
$\frac{M_2}{2}$
You mean I got that wrong too?
No! Well... yes.
Well, not so much wrong as... incomplete.

...that changed the way we think about the universe? That's general relativity.

$$F = \frac{Gm_1 m_2}{r^2}$$
THEN

Now
↓

$$R_{\mu\nu} - \frac{1}{2}g_{\mu\nu}R = \frac{8\pi G}{c^4}T_{\mu\nu}$$

It took ten years for him to complete it, and he didn't do it in a vacuum. Others, like Minkowski and Grossmann, contributed.

But "Einstein" is the household name for good reason.

The insights behind that equation are just as mind-boggling as those he had about the speed of light.

His imagination is responsible not only for the fixed speed of light, but also the elastic passage of time.

$$F = \frac{Gm_1 m_2}{r^2}$$
THEN

Nothing compels us to assume that clocks in different gravitational potentials must go at the same rate.

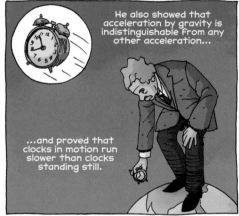

He also showed that acceleration by gravity is indistinguishable from any other acceleration...

...and proved that clocks in motion run slower than clocks standing still.

Not a lot slower... The record for human speed and duration is held by cosmonaut Sergei Avdeyev.

His 748 days at 27,360 km/hr on the Mir space station left him 0.02 seconds younger than those of us stuck on Earth while he orbited.

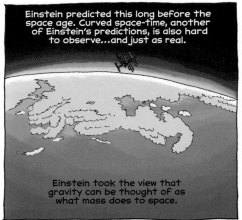

Einstein predicted this long before the space age. Curved space-time, another of Einstein's predictions, is also hard to observe...and just as real.

Einstein took the view that gravity can be thought of as what mass does to space.

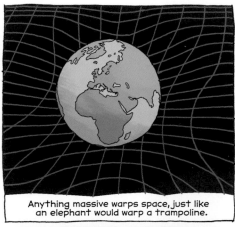

Anything massive warps space, just like an elephant would warp a trampoline.

That means even something weightless—like a photon—is affected when it gets near something massive.

So gravity changes both how time passes and how light moves. Or so he thought...

It would be urgently wished that astronomers take up the questions here raised.

Apart from any theory, is it possible, with the equipment at present available, to detect an influence of gravitational fields on the propagation of light?

He said this in 1911, so "the equipment at present available" was a telescope...

...and the Sun. The eclipsed Sun, to be more precise.

During a solar eclipse, with the Sun blotted out by the Moon, you can see light from distant stars that lie almost directly behind the Sun from our point of view on Earth.

If Einstein was right, that starlight takes a curved path to get to us because the Sun curves the space it travels through.

So the distant star would look like it's in a *different place* than when the Sun is not in its way.

The experiment Einstein urgently wished for had to wait until the world—or at least Europe—got done having a war, but on May 29, 1919, two teams of astronomers took the measurements.

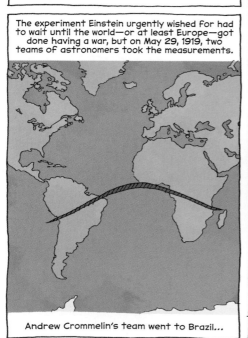

Andrew Crommelin's team went to Brazil...

...and Arthur Eddington went to Príncipe Island in the Gulf of Guinea.

The present eclipse expedition may confirm Einstein's *weird theory*, or may lead to a result of yet more far-reaching consequences—no deflection of starlight.

"Through cloud. Hopeful."

Both Crommelin and Eddington got results—Crommelin's telegram read "Eclipse splendid."

Got both your backs.

Deflection it was. And with that experimental confirmation, Albert Einstein became EINSTEIN! in the eyes of the world.

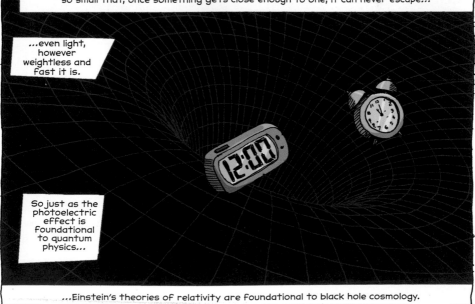

Ultimately, his theories and their consequences give us the idea of objects so massive but so small that, once something gets close enough to one, it can never escape...

...even light, however weightless and fast it is.

So just as the photoelectric effect is foundational to quantum physics...

...Einstein's theories of relativity are foundational to black hole cosmology.

Which, it may surprise you to find out, Einstein—no, wait... EINSTEIN!—found just as distasteful as quantum mechanics.

Eddington had his back on this too...

I think there should be a law of nature to prevent a star from behaving in this absurd way!

This is one case—his objection to quantum theory is another—where Einstein's sense of aesthetics led him down the wrong path.

There was yet another, but on that one he later changed his mind.

"Even Homer nods," *ja?*

Observations did the trick.

Einstein was just fine with reality teaching him a thing or two, and as we've seen, astronomers weren't idle while he was rethinking space and time for us.

They were observing things that shook up everybody's notions of how the universe began.

An even briefer history of the big bang (1928–1931)

It's traditional to start these discussions with "In the beginning..." and a tour of other creation myths.

But like many things in nature, the scientific truth is more interesting than any story we could make up.

So we'll skip mythology and stay in the 20th century.

The success of general relativity in predicting the behavior of light, and the curvature of space, came at a cost...

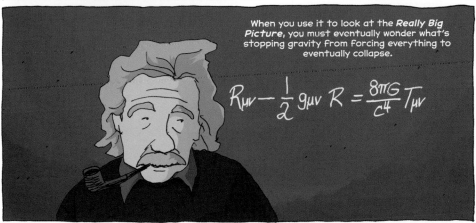

When you use it to look at the *Really Big Picture*, you must eventually wonder what's stopping gravity from forcing everything to eventually collapse.

$$R_{\mu\nu} - \frac{1}{2} g_{\mu\nu} R = \frac{8\pi G}{c^4} T_{\mu\nu}$$

Like most scientists of his time, Einstein thought the universe was *static* and *eternal*.

$$R_{\mu\nu} - \frac{1}{2} g_{\mu\nu} R$$

Thought it, preferred it...and then *fudged* his own equation to *ensure* it.

$$R_{\mu\nu} - \frac{1}{2} g_{\mu\nu} R + g_{\mu\nu}\Lambda = \frac{8\pi G}{c^4} T_{\mu\nu}$$

Einstein added a cosmological constant (Λ) to guarantee the answer came out the way he wanted it to.

49

A few scientists—very few at first—didn't share this preference for a static universe.

One was the Russian mathematician and physicist Alexander Friedmann.

FRIEDMANN

He took his cues from Einstein...

What if the speed of light in a vacuum is a constant?

What if clocks don't always run at the same speed?

What if space and time aren't separate at all?

$$R_{\mu\nu} - \frac{1}{2} g_{\mu\nu} R + \frac{8\pi G}{c^4} T_{\mu\nu}$$

Friedmann's radical "What if?"

What if the universe changes? *Evolves?*

No, nonono. *That's* going too far.

And fine-tuning a constant to make things come out the way you want them to *isn't?*

$$_{\mu\nu} R + g_{\mu\nu} \Lambda = \frac{8\pi G}{c^4}$$

Friedmann solved Einstein's field equations without picking a Λ that ensured a static, eternal universe.

The result of his work? Different kinds of curvatures for space...

The physicist and priest Lemaître took this a step further.

He argued that general relativity and quantum theory implied the universe must be expanding.

MONSEIGNEUR GEORGES HENRI JOSEPH ÉDOUARD LEMAÎTRE

He even proposed an actual origin of the universe, a real "in the beginning" that started with what he called the "primeval atom."

I think that such a beginning of the world is far enough from the present order of nature to be not at all repugnant.

Einstein didn't like this either. At all.

Your calculations are *correct*, but your physics is *atrocious*.

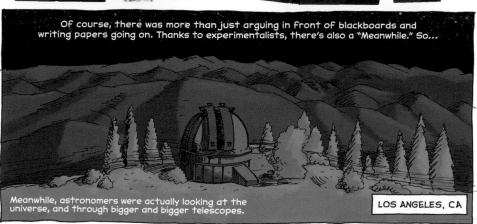

Of course, there was more than just arguing in front of blackboards and writing papers going on. Thanks to experimentalists, there's also a "Meanwhile." So...

Meanwhile, astronomers were actually looking at the universe, and through bigger and bigger telescopes.

LOS ANGELES, CA

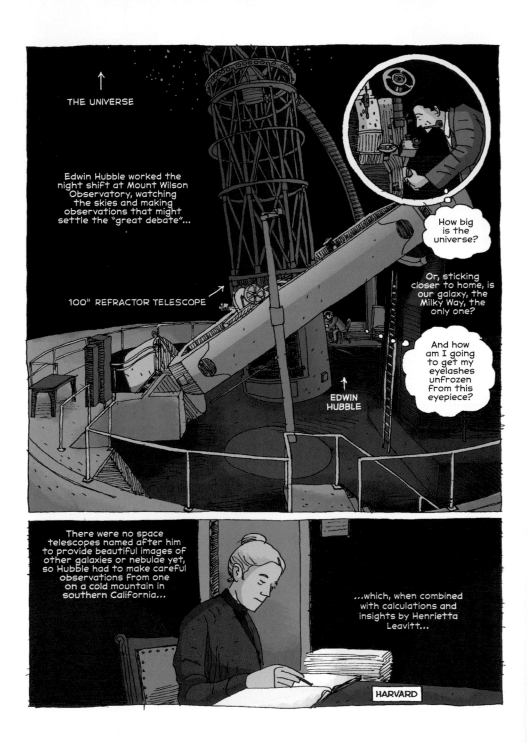

THE UNIVERSE ↑

Edwin Hubble worked the night shift at Mount Wilson Observatory, watching the skies and making observations that might settle the "great debate"...

100" REFRACTOR TELESCOPE

EDWIN HUBBLE

How big is the universe?

Or, sticking closer to home, is our galaxy, the Milky Way, the only one?

And how am I going to get my eyelashes unfrozen from this eyepiece?

There were no space telescopes named after him to provide beautiful images of other galaxies or nebulae yet, so Hubble had to make careful observations from one on a cold mountain in southern California...

...which, when combined with calculations and insights by Henrietta Leavitt...

HARVARD

...showed two things.

First, we live on a small planet, circling an ordinary star, on the outskirts of an ordinary galaxy...

...one of who-knows-how-many such galaxies.

YOU ARE HERE

Second, in the words of Douglas Adams, "Space is big. Really big. You just won't believe how vastly hugely mind-bogglingly big it is."*

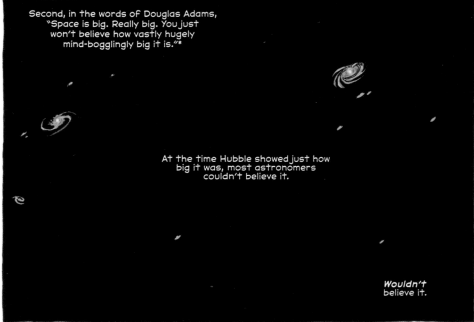

At the time Hubble showed just how big it was, most astronomers couldn't believe it.

Wouldn't believe it.

* Hubble originally estimated the distance between galaxies as 900,000 light-years. Which is still plenty far, since a light-year is 9.5 trillion km.

Douglas Adams again: "Even light, which travels so fast that it takes most races thousands of years to realize that it travels at all, takes time to journey between stars."

That's where Hubble's next big discovery came in.

Years of additional observation of stars and galaxies showed that when light travels between us and them, its wavelength *increases*.

The *farther* away the object is, the *more* the wavelength changes.

That's the Doppler effect. You're familiar with it from the way sound gets stretched out—pitched lower—as its source moves away from you.

The same thing—a shift toward redder wavelengths—happens with light coming from distant galaxies.

That means they're traveling away... In every direction Hubble looked, galaxies were traveling away from us.

The universe, then? It's *expanding*.

54

That meant Einstein's fine-tuning of the cosmological constant was not a great idea.

He wasn't as unhappy to abandon it as you might think.

Since I have introduced this term, I had always a bad conscience... I found it very ugly indeed.

And Lemaître's primeval atom?

The monseigneur dropped in on a meeting between Hubble and Einstein in February, 1931, and Einstein proved that a *good* scientist is an *open-minded* scientist.

Einstein was, of course, both.*

Yours is the most beautiful and satisfactory explanation of creation to which I have ever listened.

* He came to terms with quantum theory, though!

When theory and observation come together, science can take a great leap forward. The basis of modern cosmology was established at the Einstein-Hubble-Lemaître meeting.

$$R_{\mu\nu} - \frac{1}{2} g_{\mu\nu} R + g_{\mu\nu}\Lambda = \frac{8\pi G}{c^4} T_{\mu\nu}$$

Looking back, I can recognize it as the foundation for my own work.

Which brings us back to Fred Hoyle, who—like Einstein—had to give up on the static universe. Hoyle stuck with his steady-state idea, though.

We now come to the question of applying observational tests to theories of the expanding universe.

As I said, he was very busy being a public scientist.

These theories are based on the hypothesis that all matter in the universe was created at a particular time in the remote past in one...

ssss ssssssss

Can you cut out that static hiss in the background?

..."big bang"?

The degree to which this, this..."theory"... *conflicts* with observation can *hardly* be ignored.

Can't seem to get rid of it. Sorry.

BBC

He coined the phrase "Big Bang" thinking people would use it contemptuously— that's how *he* meant it.

No such luck. But that didn't deter him, nor did it deter Sciama.

I'm with Hoyle, of course. He says "a new way must be found," and that new way is the steady-state universe.

Expanding, but with matter continuously created to keep everything in balance.

Dennis was also interested in Mach's principle.

...don't suppose they teach it now, but it's terribly interesting. The idea is that the inertia of an object arises from all the other matter in the universe.

Einstein had coined the name, and used this principle as a guide to construct general relativity.

...Turns out Einstein later disowned it, but I think he was mistaken to do so.

I couldn't say that to him in so many words, of course.

Wait, you met... Einstein?

Just before he died. I was quite nervous.

But I knew he had a sense of humor, so I started out with a joke...

Professor Einstein, I've come to talk about Mach's principle.

And I've come to defend your former self against your later self.

Ho, ho, ho, that is good. *Ja!*

So then I talked about *my* ideas, and he talked about his work and his doubts about quantum theory and so on.

That is good. *Ja!*

I thought "later Einstein" was right to abandon Mach's principle. But even though I disagreed with Dennis on many such things, our discussions stimulated me to develop my own picture.

Are you all right there, Hawking?

And the picture that was emerging included many strange new ideas.

For instance, collapsed stars... something Einstein also didn't like. Not that the universe cares *who* likes *what*.

Again, Einstein, Hubble, and Lemaître's accord became the foundation for my own work.

What happened?

Fine. Jus' snagged my foot on something.

I just didn't realize it at the time.

In fact, in my first term at Cambridge, I was rather bored.

Not even physics seemed to be worth doing.

58

Jane (December 1962)

I was back home in St. Albans after the Michaelmas term when two events transpired that—eventually—changed that attitude.

The first event didn't seem significant at the time.

...and I needed that First to go on to graduate study at Cambridge.

It was a near thing, so I demanded a viva.

I knew the idea of infecting Cambridge with the likes of me was all too tempting.

So I told them that if they gave me a First, I'd leave, and if not, well...

They could look forward to *many more years* of me right there at Oxford.

"And then I said..."

I wager you'll give me that First.

"I didn't even make it to the door before they had their decision."

Mr. Hawking, wait.

And off to Cambridge I went!

That is so totally, completely, and utterly...

...implausible.

There's not an Oxford don in the history of Oxford dons that can think or decide on anything that fast. Nor are you anywhere *near* that bold.

Nonono, I assure you!

And I did have a backup plan. I was going to take the Civil Service exam. But then I forgot to go take the test...

Well, *that* part sounds plausible, anyway. Do you show up for classes now, at least?

And how's this Sciama fellow?

Well, our ideas about cosmology differ a great deal.

But I don't know. I suppose he's fine.

Er.

What's cosmology, then?

60

Jane, wasn't it?

You're reading in languages at university, right?

Well, I plan to. This coming autumn.

Oh, right. Then from the Greek—"cosmology" would be study of the world.

So, like... geography?

No, nothing so small as that. It's about the universe, really.

Ah. Greek by way of Latin and French, then—"cosmos" as in "order."

If you say so. Einstein, Hoyle...that lot. Plenty of math.

Which I suppose I had better study properly, now.

You, study? I'd like to see that!

Well, maybe I should just teach it instead, then.

Speaking of which, might you teach me your address? I'm Stephen, by the way.

We danced some, and I invited her to my 21st birthday party, which was a few days later.

She accepted!

Jane, isn't it? Come in, please, do come in.

This is my father, Dr. Frank Hawking.

Pleasure to meet you, Dr. Hawking.

Father, Ms. Jane Wilde.

Mother, this is Jane Wilde. She's just finishing up at St Albans.

It's a pleasure to meet you.

It certainly is. St Albans, you say?

Oh my. I always wondered who *these* people were, and now...

Well, yes. St Albans High School. I begin at Westfield College, University of London, this autumn.

The party was a success.

Graduate students and doctors and people with...with *jobs.*

And even with all these people, so cold in here! I should just...

Well, not a total success.

People thought I'd had a bit too much that night, but...

...I, unfortunately, knew better.

Thank you for keeping me company, Edward.

I think I must be going.

Don't let that worry you. Happens all the time.

And besides, Edward seems to like you.

Thank you for coming, and thank you for the record token. There's a new recording out of Wagner's *Siegfried* that I would very much like to have.

Edward likes me? Ah well.

Not multiple sclerosis (1963)

The second event that changed my attitude toward...everything... occurred out on Verulamium Pond not long after.

Did you hurt yourself, Stephen?

...

No.

THUMP

Come on, then. It's cold.

I...

Can you please help me up?

Help you...

Mary, Philippa! Edward? Come here please?

Stephen and I shall go to a café to warm up, I think. Mary, please watch after your brother and sister.

Mother. I don't need minding.

Of course you don't. But Edward does, so help your sister keep an eye on him.

I told her about some other incidents in the last year or so. Slurred speech, tripping, trouble on stairs. That sort of thing.

Well, so you've fallen a few times.

Dear, if you must know...you've *always* been rather clumsy.

No, this is different.

Today is an example, and not the only one in recent months. I've had a hard time with my shoelaces and neckties now and again, and...

Well then. You must see a doctor.

No, I...

I *insist* you see a doctor.

So I did.

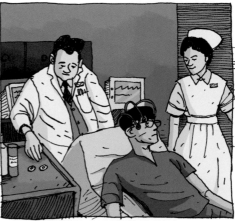
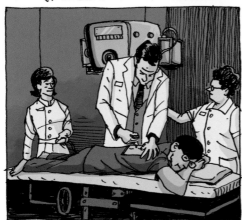

After all that, they didn't tell me what I had,
though they ruled out multiple sclerosis.

I didn't press for details...

...because they were obviously bad.

I was home for a few more weeks, and word got out. Basil's sister told Jane.

...quite mad, you know.

Not mad. Eccentric. And I rather like eccentric.

Oh! Have you heard?

No, what? Why? I haven't heard anything.

Well, apparently Stephen's been in the hospital for two weeks—Burt's I think, because that's where his father trained and where Mary's training now.

You mightn't have noticed, but he'd been stumbling and couldn't tie his shoelaces.

They did lots of horrible tests, apparently, and he's suffering from some terrible, paralyzing, incurable disease.

It's a bit like multiple sclerosis, but it's not. They reckon he's probably only got a couple of years...

Are you all right?

Yes. No. I don't...

Bit of a shock, that's all. We're—to go on a date tomorrow.

Italian dinner in Soho. Then *Volpone* at the Old Vic. And...

I don't know.

Should I beg off?

Well, like I said, the whole family's mad, but my brother Basil adores him.

And you like the theatre. And *him* besides, yes?

You should go.

We had a fine evening, but it proved a bit beyond my means.

I was out of money before we made it to the bus going home.

Er. This is terribly embarrassing, but...can you pay, um, this fare?

Of course, I... No!

No! I-I've lost my money purse!

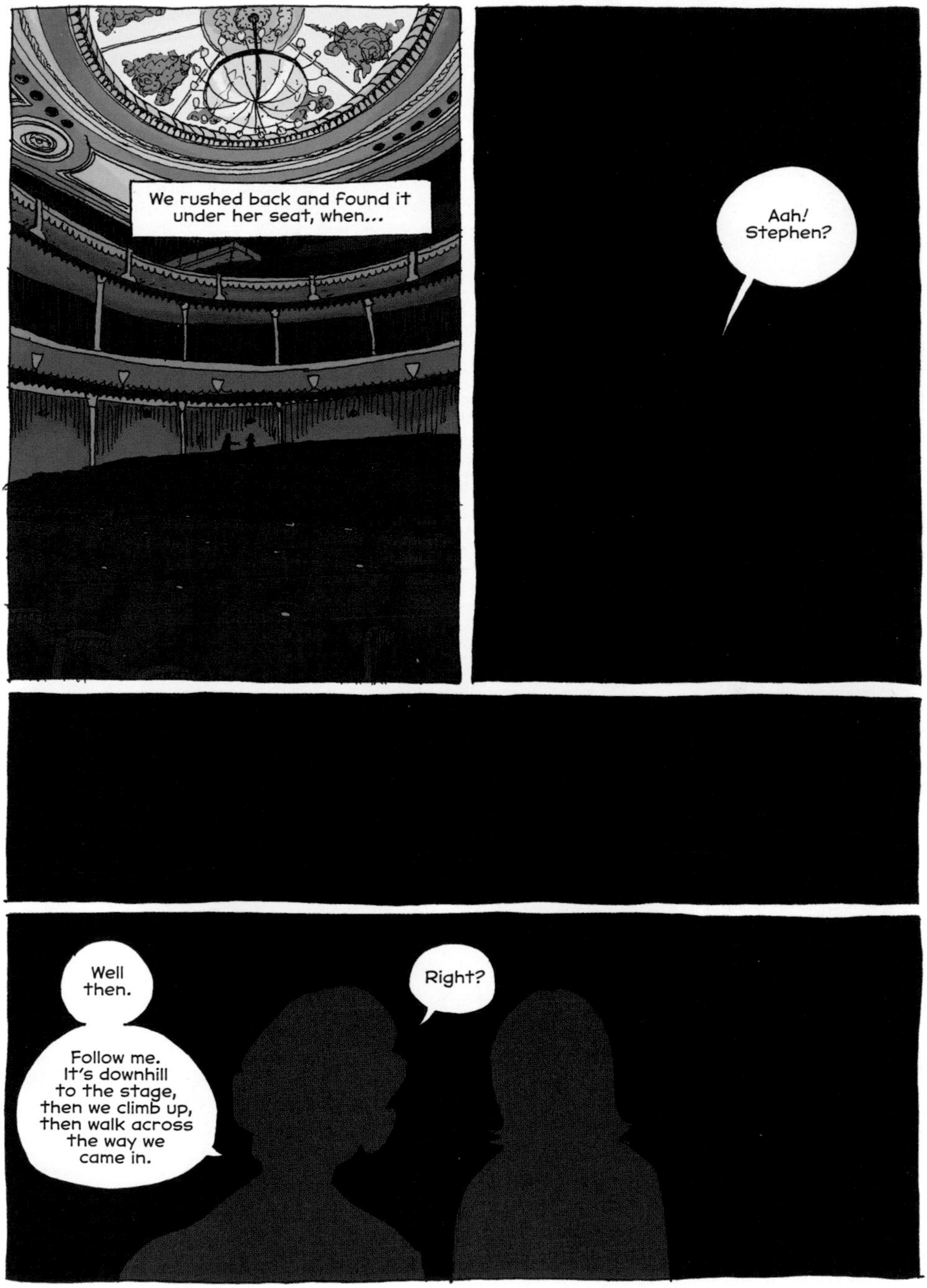
We rushed back and found it under her seat, when...
Aah! Stephen?
Well then.
Follow me. It's downhill to the stage, then we climb up, then walk across the way we came in.
Right?

Right.

We know where we are, and where we're going.

Nothing to worry about. And we're onstage at the Old Vic!

We groped our way down, then up, and then out.

Nothing else, there in the dark?

...

Diana! No! Perfect gentleman.

What I was *going* to say was he may not dance well any longer...

He never danced *well*, Jane. Just vigorously.

Who's talking to *you*, anyway? Go on...

Be that as it may, what I was going to say is he leads rather well.

Lovely grey eyes, and a lovely smile too.

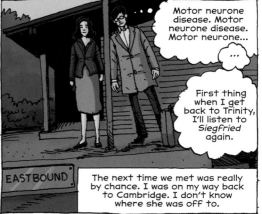

Motor neurone disease. Motor neurone disease. Motor neurone...

...

First thing when I get back to Trinity, I'll listen to *Siegfried* again.

EASTBOUND

The next time we met was really by chance. I was on my way back to Cambridge. I don't know where she was off to.

...and I still feel awkward about the bus fare.

You paid me back—think nothing of it.

Well. Thank you.

How...

How are you feeling, if I might ask?

Fine.

I mean, it's all right if—

Everything's fine.

Would you like to go to Trinity Hall's May Ball* with me?

I. Yes.

Yes, I would.

* Held in June, in true Cambridge fashion.

Right. Very good. I'll see you in June.

Yes. Until then!

Motor neurone disease. Motor neurone disease. Motor neurone disease.

It was hard to focus on the future, really.

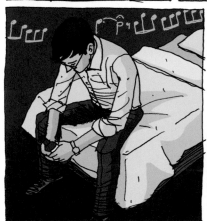

What was the point?

Later reports said I drank heavily.

An exaggeration. I did listen to a great deal of Wagner, though.

"My dreams at that time were rather disturbed." (1963)

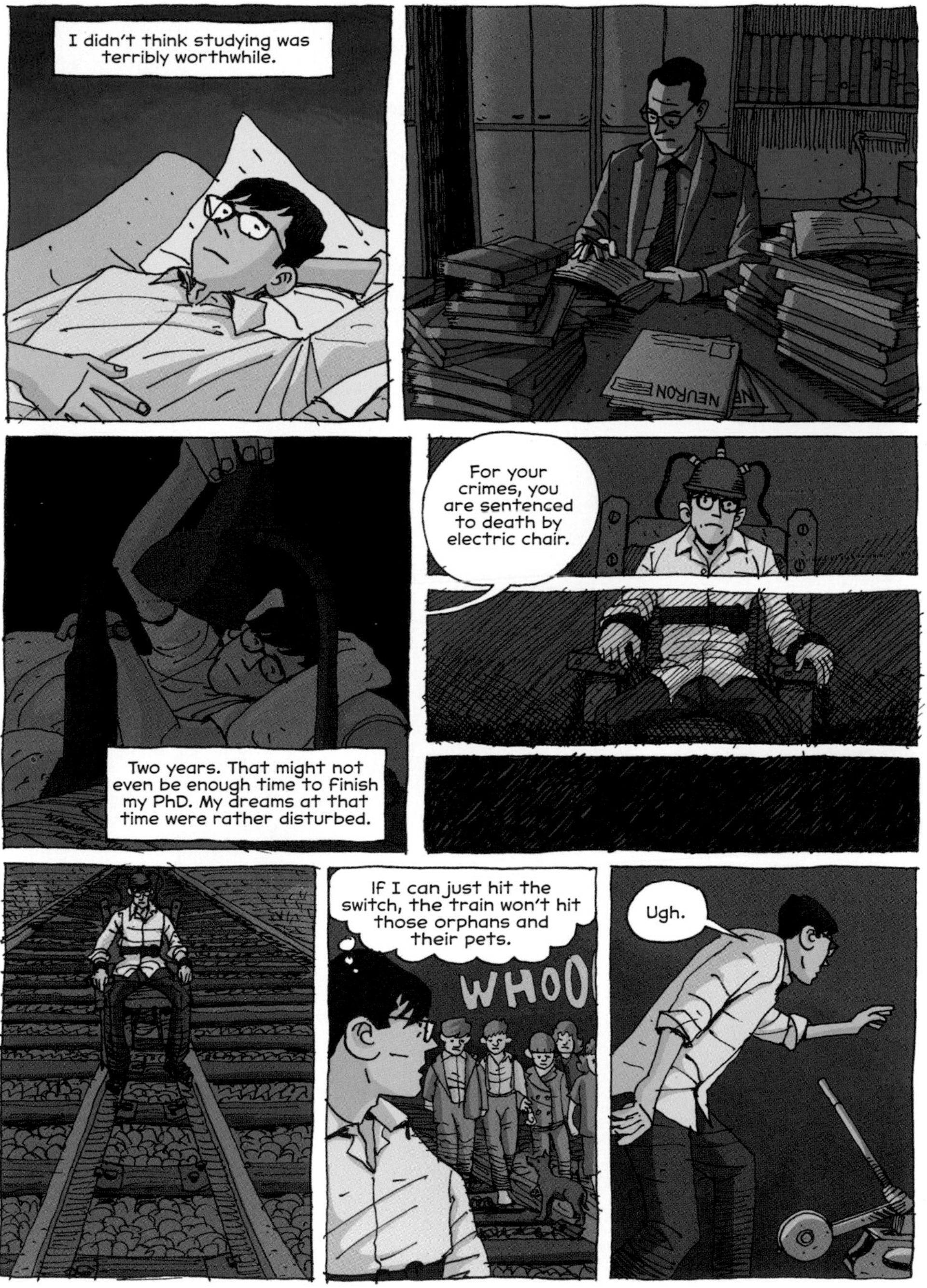

I didn't think studying was terribly worthwhile.
NEURON
Two years. That might not even be enough time to finish my PhD. My dreams at that time were rather disturbed.
For your crimes, you are sentenced to death by electric chair.
If I can just hit the switch, the train won't hit those orphans and their pets.
WHOO
Ugh.

Troubled and recurring, as it turns out.

I considered myself a tragic character—

—perhaps others did too, when I told them.

Oh. I thought you might have a speech impediment of some sort.

Is there anything that can be done?

No. Motor neurone disease is rare...

...there wasn't much known about it.

Two years at most was the medical consensus. I'd lose all voluntary muscle control.

I'd be able to blink and smile—a major part of smiling involves involuntary muscles...

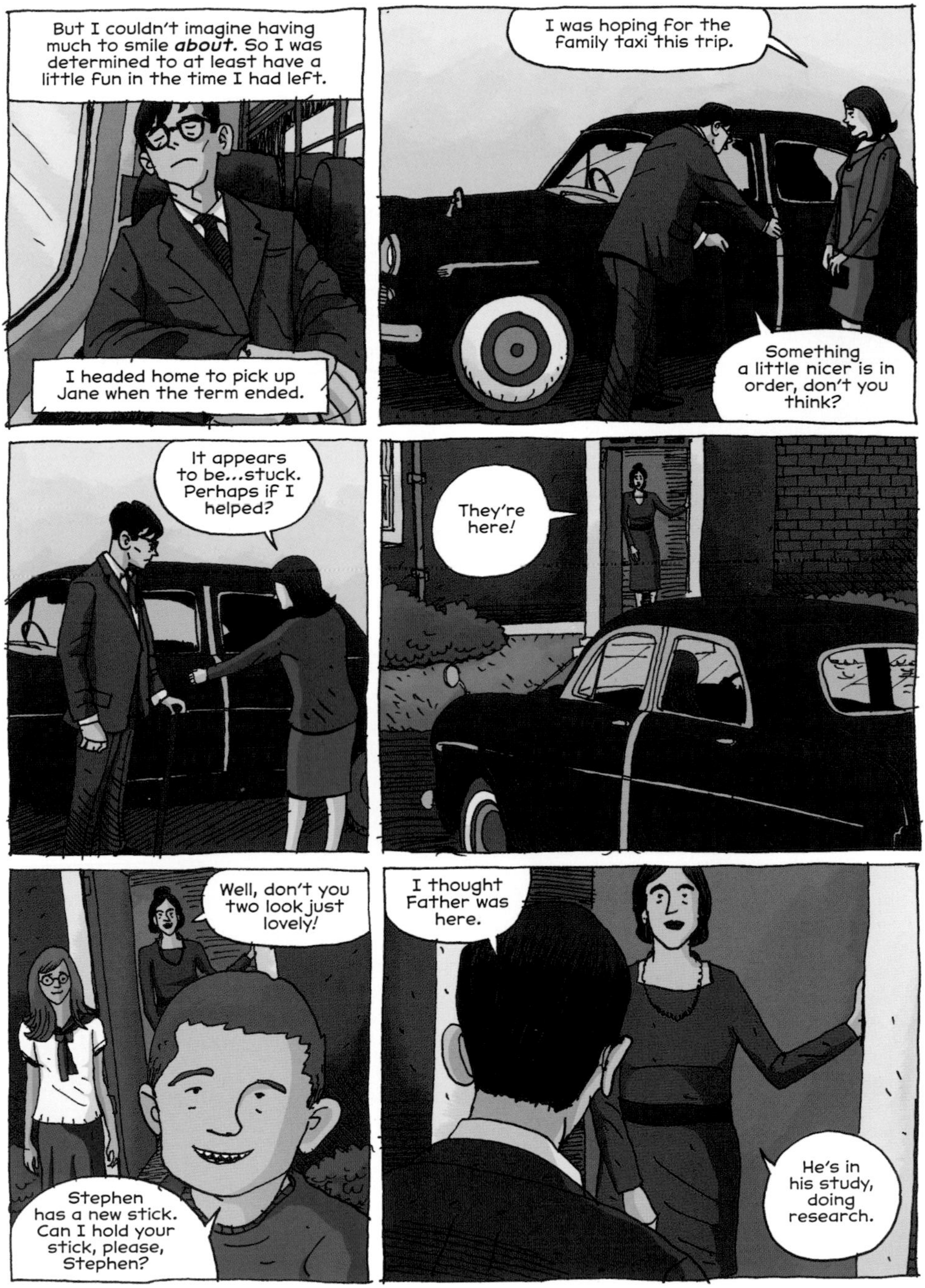
But I couldn't imagine having much to smile *about*. So I was determined to at least have a little fun in the time I had left.
I headed home to pick up Jane when the term ended.
I was hoping for the family taxi this trip.
Something a little nicer is in order, don't you think?
It appears to be...stuck. Perhaps if I helped?
They're here!
Well, don't you two look just lovely!
Stephen has a new stick. Can I hold your stick, please, Stephen?
I thought Father was here.
He's in his study, doing research.

Oh. Of course.

Well, I'll be back tomorrow.

Are you going to tell him what you've found out about his disease?

Once I've worked out a regimen, yes. This letter from Dr. Wilson provides some insight, and Dr. Thomson says sublingual therapy might be effective. Here I've learned that...

...umm, it's Calmic Ltd. that has a new drug, and that fellow Walton at Newcastle General—remember him?—had some advice. I'm writing the University of Wales shortly too.

Well, as long as there's progress.

Nothing definite. But there are things we can try.

The consensus is there will be no pain, at least. Just a loss of muscular control over... everything, eventually.

But many victims suffer from depression, or panic. Did you notice...

Frank. He's off to the May Ball, and with a lovely girl. I shouldn't think so!

Perhaps... we... could...

slow...

URK

...down?

We could, yes, but there's no time, and we don't want to be late.

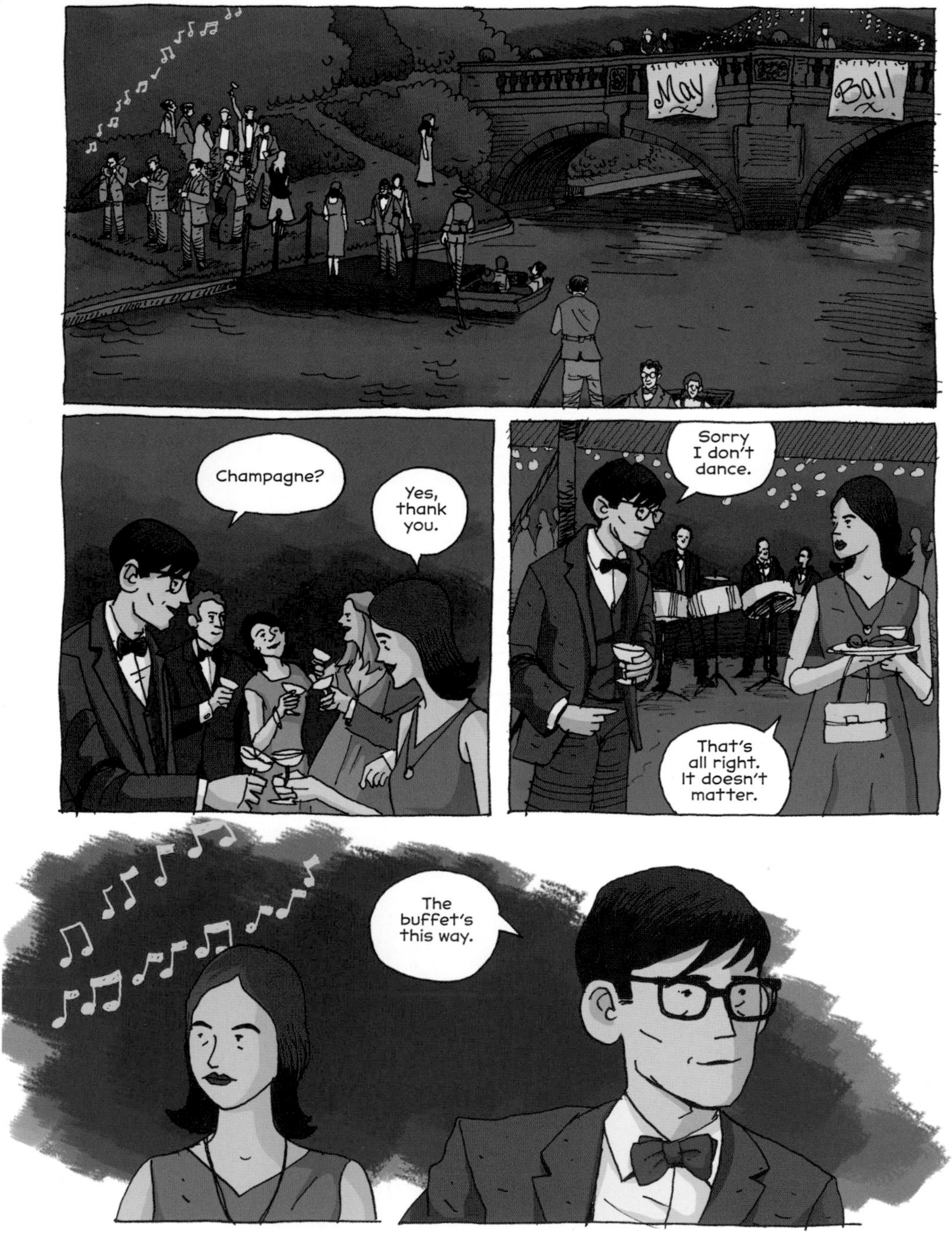
May
Ball
Champagne?
Yes, thank you.
Sorry I don't dance.
That's all right. It doesn't matter.
The buffet's this way.

Hawking's here.

Steve! Come on over and tell Jayant that foolish idea you had about Wheeler-Feynman electrodynamics.

No, downstairs. I want to see if the jazz band is any good.

...Nonono. I assure you it's a good deal less foolish than your hypothesis.

GEORGE ELLIS

Frankly, your notions are daft.

—never give it a rest, do they?

Like a bunch of football hooligans, but about physics.

Oh, look. You can see only the men's cuffs and collars.

The math won't support it.

Not so surprising.

81

The light is picking up the fluorescents in the laundry powder.

Most of the girls' dresses are new, like yours... haven't been subjected to detergent.

Shall we go out to the dance floor and make sure?

I thought you said... Of course. Thank you, Sidney.

Not so fast, Steve, and none of this lecturing me on math. Save it for your undergrads.

I shall, George, I shall. But you might benefit from my tutelage as well. Now, if you'll excuse us...

I've started tutoring. It's the best way I've found of learning the stuff I...omitted during my own undergraduate work.

The students are appallingly *unmotivated*, though.

Anyway, if we're going to talk about this more, you fellows will have to fetch us some champagne after this number.

SLIP

Perhaps that will serve to make those ideas of yours more palatable.

Whoa, are you all right, there? Here, I'll get us all another round.

STUMBLE

You must be tired. Just take it easy. I'll help George, and we'll be back in no time.

Please please me (1963)

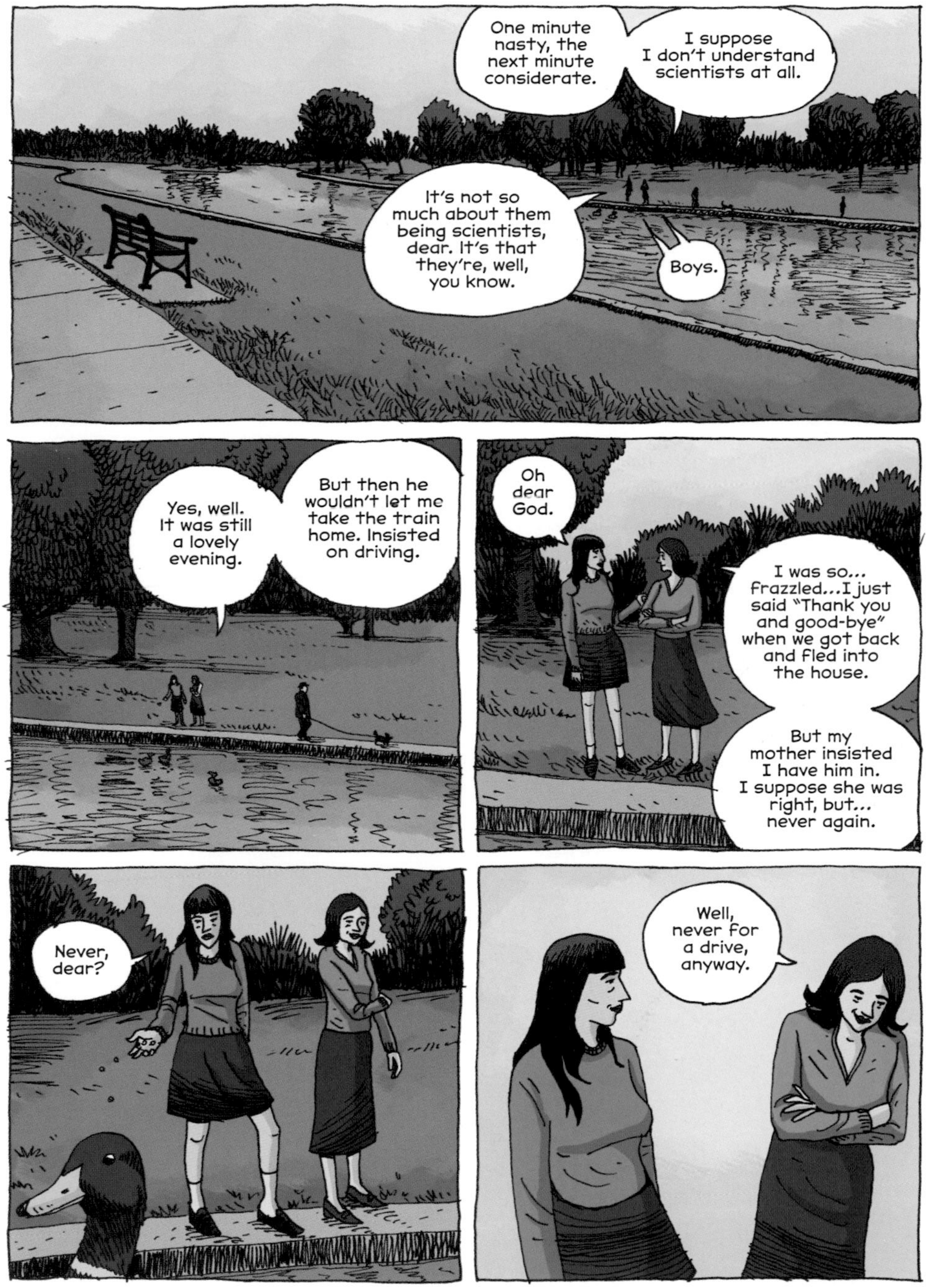

One minute nasty, the next minute considerate.
I suppose I don't understand scientists at all.
It's not so much about them being scientists, dear. It's that they're, well, you know.
Boys.
Yes, well. It was still a lovely evening.
But then he wouldn't let me take the train home. Insisted on driving.
Oh dear God.
I was so... frazzled...I just said "Thank you and good-bye" when we got back and fled into the house.
But my mother insisted I have him in. I suppose she was right, but... never again.
Never, dear?
Well, never for a drive, anyway.

Around that time I found myself interested in the elegies of John Donne.

"When thou art there, consider what this chase/ Misspent by thy beginning at the face."

??

That surprised my friends, along with my listening to less Wagner and more "Pick of the Pops" on Radio Luxembourg.

...SO HARD TO REASON WITH YO WHOA YEAH...

As did the realization that there were things I wanted to do.

Jayant.

Can you tell me more about your Wheeler-Feynman work in expanding universes?

Happy to!

But the really important thing is Hoyle and I have created a time-symmetric theory of gravity for the steady-state universe.

Let me show you.

He did.

$$\sum_n \frac{E_n^{n+}(x,t) - E}{2}$$

And it was *interesting*.

"I worked it out." (1964–1965)

Not long after, we all went to a talk Hoyle gave at the Royal Society about their results. There was much excitement.

...The big bang has all the dignity and elegance of a party girl jumping out of a birthday cake.

HA HA HAH

What I *meant* is that it has *none*.

As the BBC listeners among you know, I liken our previous position to that of mountain climbers attempting a summit via multiple routes.

We found that all of them peter out on hopeless precipices.

So, many years ago, I proposed a new hypothesis—that matter is created continuously.

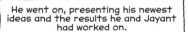

STEADY STATE

He went on, presenting his newest ideas and the results he and Jayant had worked on.

Results that had not been reviewed by anybody except Jay...

...and me.

...QED. Are there any questions?

The conclusion of his talk caused a bit of a stir.

Yes, you there.

The... the influence of matter in a steady-state universe would...

The quantities you're talking about would diverge.

That's not a question.

Of course they don't diverge.

Who is that?

Er, yes.

The masses would be infinite, which is...

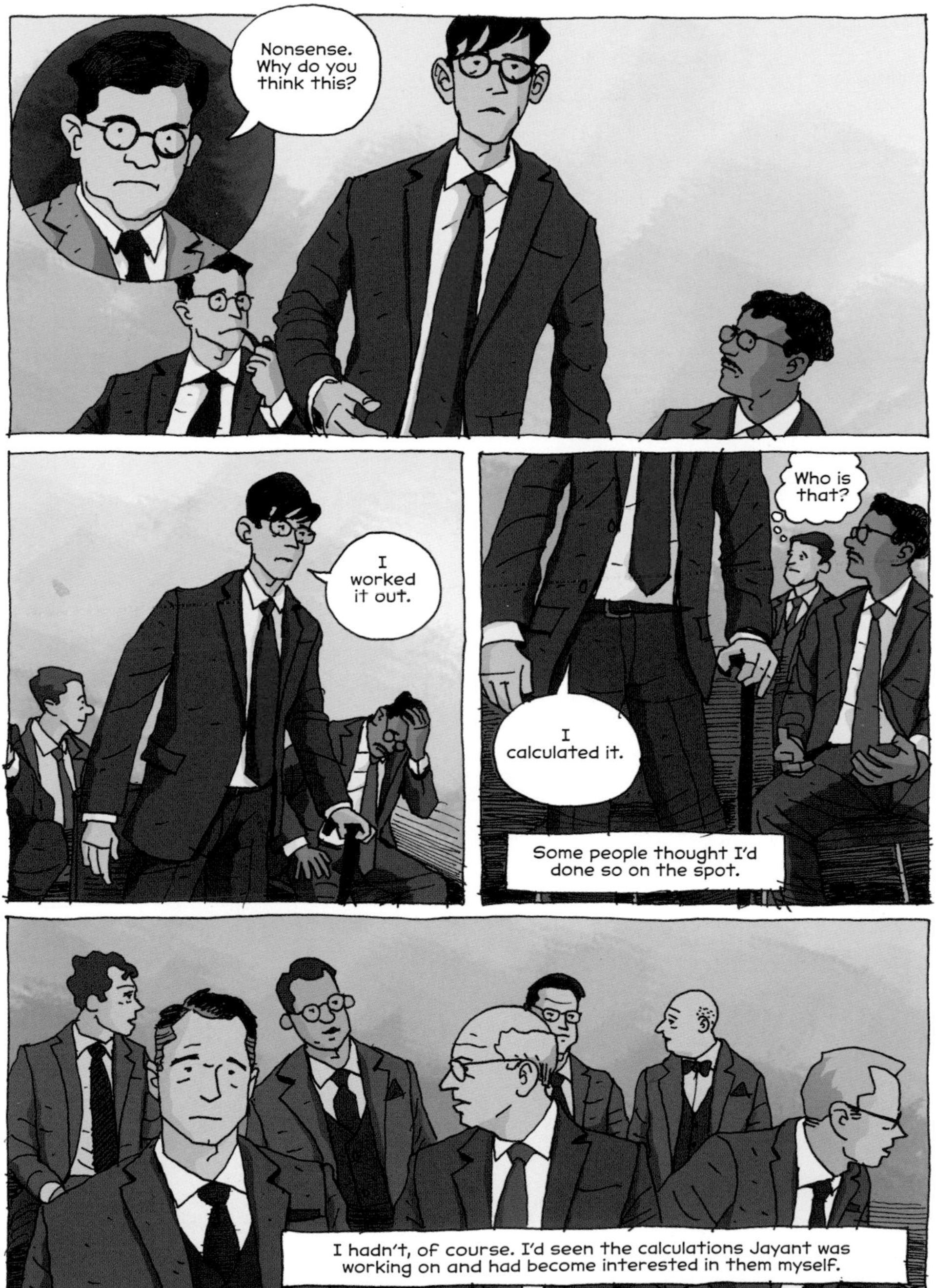
Nonsense. Why do you think this?
I worked it out.
Who is that?
I calculated it.
Some people thought I'd done so on the spot.
I hadn't, of course. I'd seen the calculations Jayant was working on and had become interested in them myself.

Regardless, this didn't hurt my reputation.

...I just wish you'd said something sooner.

Yes, well. I suppose I should have. 'M sorry about that.

And Hoyle later gave me a job, so even that turned out all right in the end.

I also began seeing more of Jane, off and on in London...

Just here for some dental work. But I thought we might go to the opera?

...between terms back home in St. Albans...

Could you turn that down so we can talk?

Why? I mean, I suppose.

...and after trips abroad for both of us.

Oh dear, what has happened?

Knocked them out in a Fall on a train in Germany.

How dreadful! And after all those special trips to that London dentist.

Yes. Those. Well, I'm glad of the trips all the same. How was Spain? Italy?

Er... how are you?

In sum, I was starting to think there might be things worth doing.

Very interesting results, these. Penrose presented them at a seminar in London.

Perhaps you...

I didn't attend. Other engagement.

But I heard about it.

The disease had slowed, and I had gotten interested in collapsing stars and Roger Penrose's singularity ideas...

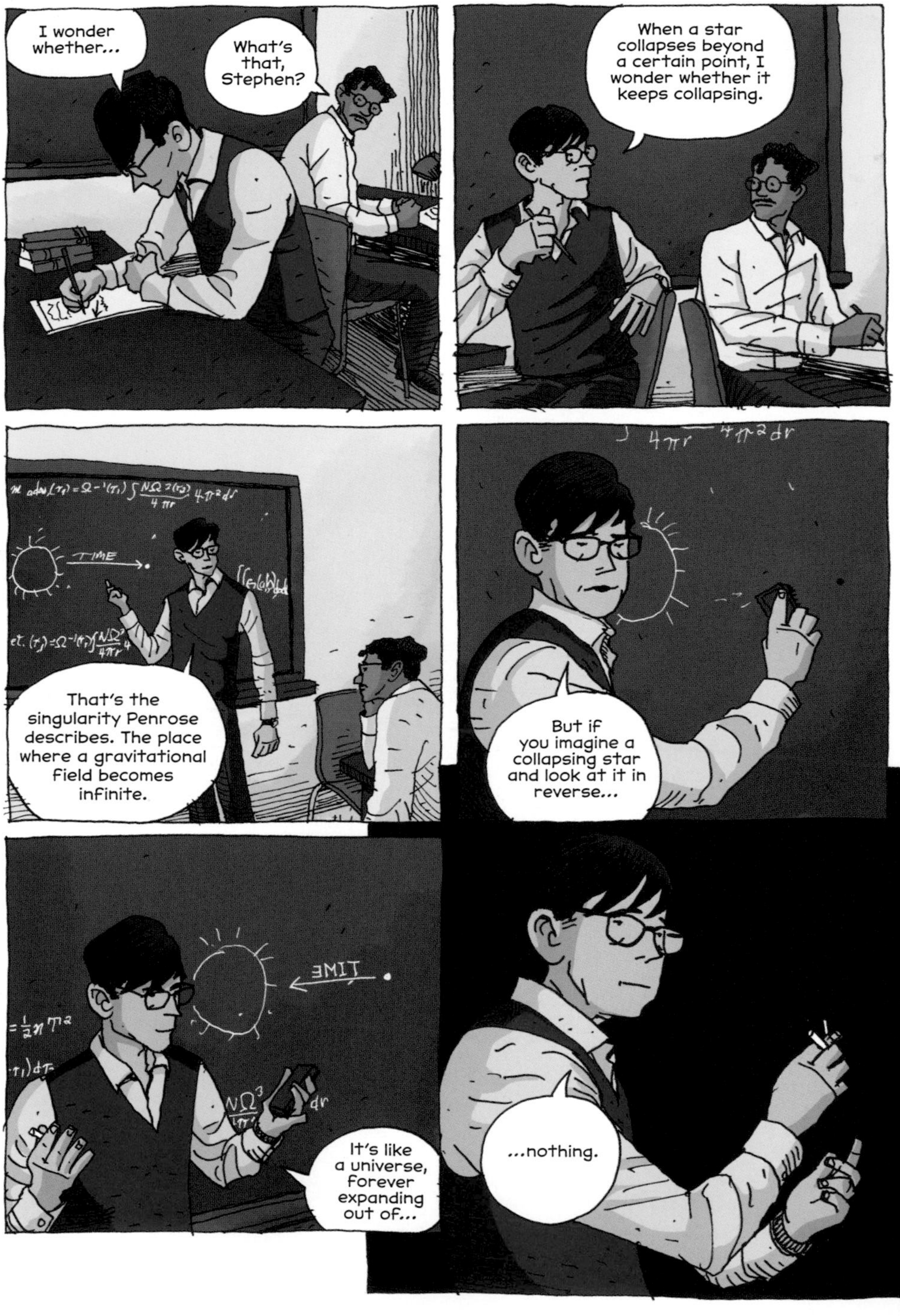
I wonder whether...
What's that, Stephen?
When a star collapses beyond a certain point, I wonder whether it keeps collapsing.
That's the singularity Penrose describes. The place where a gravitational field becomes infinite.
But if you imagine a collapsing star and look at it in reverse...
It's like a universe, forever expanding out of...
...nothing.

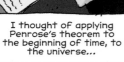
I thought of applying Penrose's theorem to the beginning of time, to the universe...

...so I eventually hit upon the notion that mightn't the reverse of a collapsing star look very much like a big bang? *The* big bang?

I think I might include that in my thesis.

Well, that sounds terribly exciting.

However—and I don't know if you've noticed—it's raining. Tell me more, but out of the elements, perhaps?

Yes. But first...

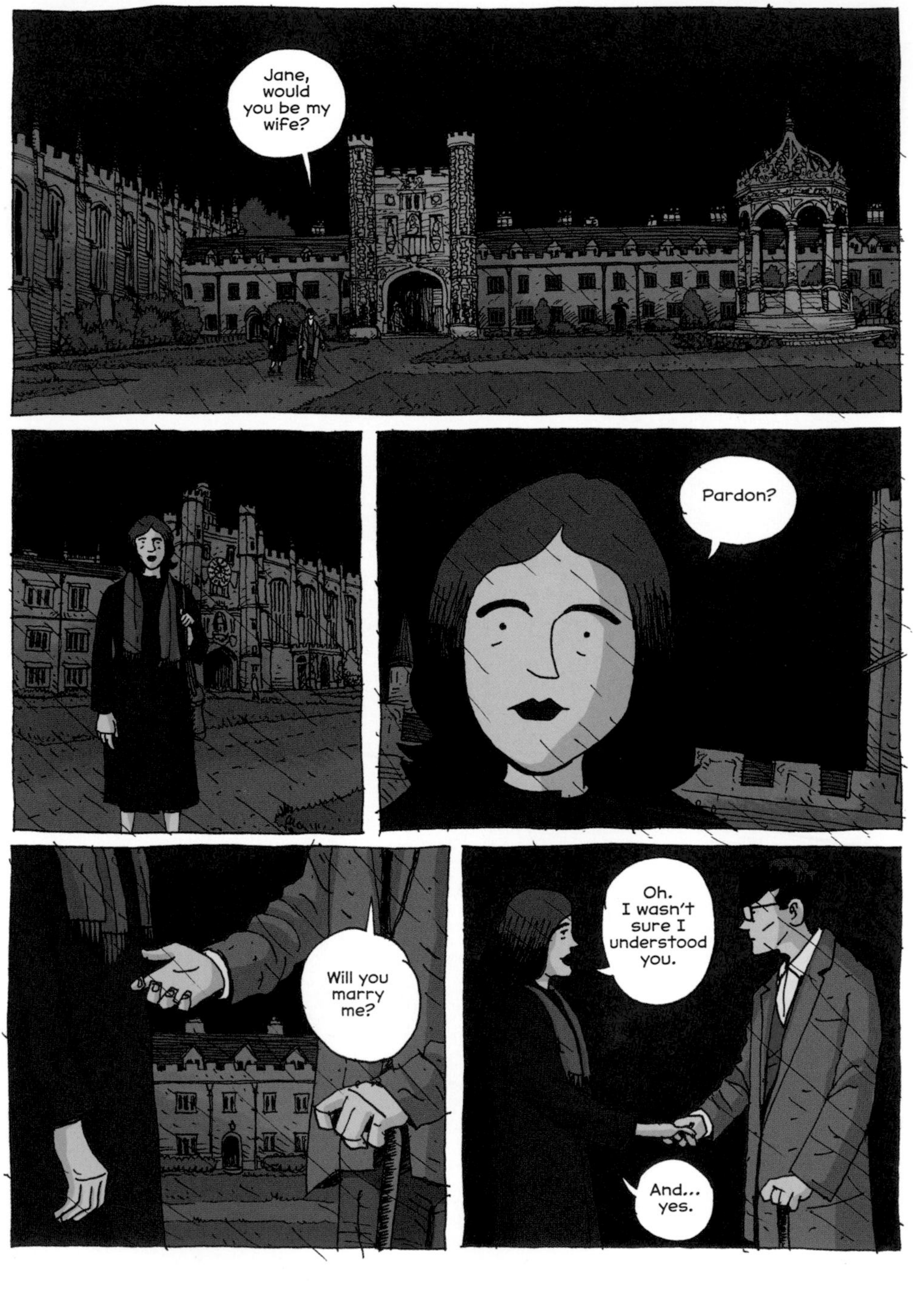
Jane, would you be my wife?
Pardon?
Will you marry me?
Oh. I wasn't sure I understood you.
And... yes.

We married in July of 1965. We had two ceremonies, actually—one civil and one a little more traditional in Trinity Hall Chapel.

A little closer together, please.

By then, I was finishing my PhD thesis.

Stephen, I can't make heads nor tails of this.

Well, I can explain the calculations again, but I really don't...

No, I can't read your *handwriting*, Stephen.

Its last chapter contained my first attempt at a theorem for the beginning of the universe.

I really think we need to talk about—

Not now. Here, let me see.

Hmm. Ahh.

Well. Okay.

I...think I'm saying the following...

It adapted Penrose's methods for calculating what would happen if a star collapsed.

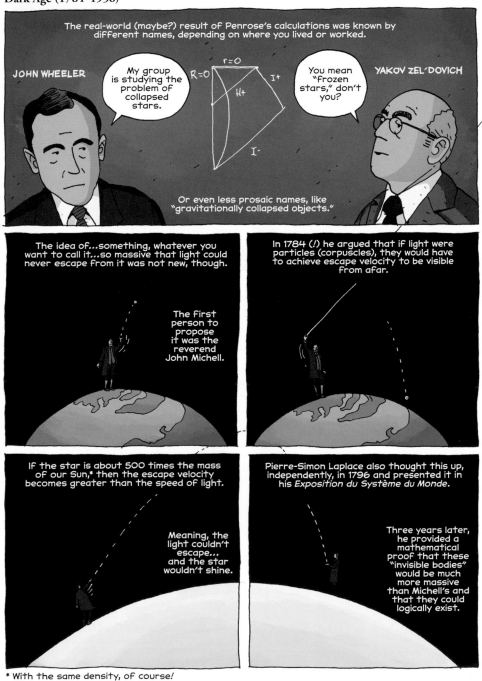

The real-world (maybe?) result of Penrose's calculations was known by different names, depending on where you lived or worked.

JOHN WHEELER

My group is studying the problem of collapsed stars.

You mean "frozen stars," don't you?

YAKOV ZEL'DOVICH

Or even less prosaic names, like "gravitationally collapsed objects."

The idea of...something, whatever you want to call it...so massive that light could never escape from it was not new, though.

The first person to propose it was the reverend John Michell.

In 1784 (!) he argued that if light were particles (corpuscles), they would have to achieve escape velocity to be visible from afar.

If the star is about 500 times the mass of our Sun,* then the escape velocity becomes greater than the speed of light.

Meaning, the light couldn't escape... and the star wouldn't shine.

Pierre-Simon Laplace also thought this up, independently, in 1796 and presented it in his *Exposition du Système du Monde*.

Three years later, he provided a mathematical proof that these "invisible bodies" would be much more massive than Michell's and that they could logically exist.

* With the same density, of course!

94

Over the next 100-plus years, their groundbreaking, astonishing, radical ideas were...

...forgotten. **Completely** uninfluential.

Theory—specifically Einstein's—and observation were nowhere near ready to test out these ideas in the real world.

The real universe.

$$R_{\mu\nu} - \frac{1}{2}g_{\mu\nu}\,F$$

But things happened fast once general relativity hit the scene.

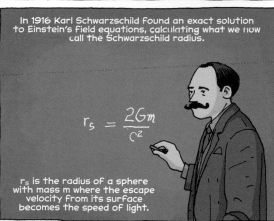

In 1916 Karl Schwarzschild found an exact solution to Einstein's field equations, calculating what we now call the Schwarzschild radius.

$$r_s = \frac{2Gm}{c^2}$$

r_s is the radius of a sphere with mass m where the escape velocity from its surface becomes the speed of light.

r_s for Earth = 0.8 cm, giving a new meaning to the phrase "blue marble."

But if the Earth was compressed to marble size, we wouldn't—couldn't!—see it as blue.

As Michell and Laplace and now Schwarzschild showed, no light of **any** color could escape.

For his solution, Schwarzschild simplified things—beyond just assuming a perfect sphere could exist, that is!

In addition to no irregularities, the massive sphere he imagined had no charge and no spin.

Not very realistic, since real planets and stars are lumpy,* have charge, and rotate.

(* The Earth actually deviates very little [less than 0.5%] from a perfect sphere, but if you've ever walked up a hill or fallen down stairs, you know it does deviate!)

Reissner and Nordström figured out how to deal with electric charge by 1918.

Dealing with spinning bodies took a lot longer.

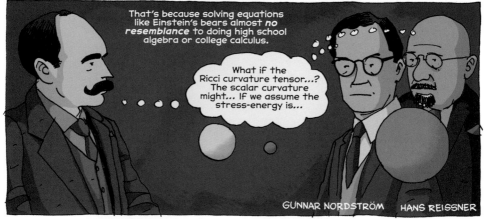

That's because solving equations like Einstein's bears almost *no resemblance* to doing high school algebra or college calculus.

What if the Ricci curvature tensor...? The scalar curvature might... If we assume the stress-energy is...

GUNNAR NORDSTRÖM   HANS REISSNER

At this level, math is as much art as it is anything else.

You have to imagine the kind of universe you're describing...

...usually a simplified version, perhaps full of perfect, uncharged, and nonrotating spheres...

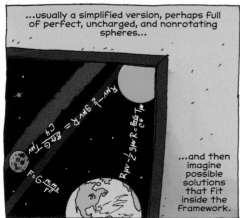

...and then imagine possible solutions that fit inside the framework.

The "=" sign means the solution must fit perfectly. No coloring outside the lines allowed.

And you have to show other artists—other scientists—exactly how you did it.

Just trust me—it works out.

And...and And AND!

Your solution needs to match up with reality—or point to a way that reality ought to match up with it—by suggesting experiments that others can perform to verify your work.

As Eddington and Crommelin found out while trying to verify Einstein's theories, those experiments will be hard to do.

Nobody said art or science was easy.

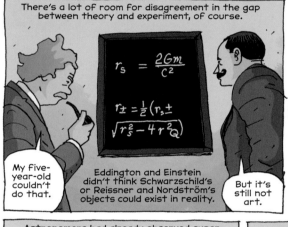

There's a lot of room for disagreement in the gap between theory and experiment, of course.

$$r_s = \frac{2Gm}{c^2}$$

$$r_{\pm} = \frac{1}{2}\left(r_s \pm \sqrt{r_s^2 - 4r_Q^2}\right)$$

My five-year-old couldn't do that.

Eddington and Einstein didn't think Schwarzschild's or Reissner and Nordström's objects could exist in reality.

But it's still not art.

The math was fine, actually—their objections were largely on aesthetic grounds.

But there were signs that the universe—already strange because of Einstein's warped space and slowed clocks—is stranger the harder we look.

Astronomers had already observed super-dense stars, called white dwarfs.

And when white dwarfs cool, by giving off radiation, they ought to shrink. All the way down past the Schwarzschild radius.

$$r_s = \frac{2Gm}{c^2}$$

$$= \frac{1}{2}(r_s \pm$$

$$-4r_Q^2)$$

Logical... unless, like Einstein, you reject the idea of "gravitationally collapsed objects" out of hand.

What's to stop the collapse?

In short, quantum mechanical laws. A young physicist, Subrahmanyan Chandrasekhar, proved it.

Where does this madness end?

But in solving the mystery of what happens to white dwarfs, he showed that more massive stars have a different fate.

$$M_{limit} = \frac{\omega_3^0 \sqrt{3\pi}}{2} \frac{\left(\frac{\hbar c}{G}\right)^{3/2}}{\frac{1}{(\mu_e m_H)^2}}$$

They collapse, maybe all the way down to a singularity.

No surprise—the old guard didn't like this.

I think there should be a law of nature to prevent a star from behaving in this absurd way!

Eddington also went on to criticize how Chandrasekhar combined special relativity with quantum mechanics to achieve his result.

I do not regard the offspring of such a union as born in lawful wedlock.

In 1939, Einstein weighed in...

The essential result of my investigation is a clear understanding as to why the "Schwarzschild singularities" do not exist in physical reality.

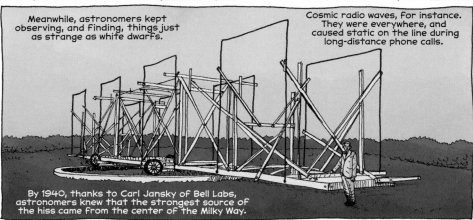

Meanwhile, astronomers kept observing, and finding, things just as strange as white dwarfs.

Cosmic radio waves, for instance. They were everywhere, and caused static on the line during long-distance phone calls.

By 1940, thanks to Carl Jansky of Bell Labs, astronomers knew that the strongest source of the hiss came from the center of the Milky Way.

99

But some originated elsewhere, and an amateur—Grote Reber—built, in his mother's backyard, the first dedicated radio telescope capable of detecting them.*

Chandrasekhar, now at the University of Chicago's observatory, had never heard of Reber but had an open mind. Some professional astronomers visited.

You did this all yourself?

Yeah, sure, how else?

His instrument and observations were impressive, and in 1940 Chandrasekhar, by then the editor of the *Astrophysical Journal*, published Reber's papers.

(* Apparently there were no zoning ordinances against such things in the Chicago suburbs.)

Reber had mapped strong radio sources in the center of our galaxy, plus two others as well.

Too little is known about cosmic static to read a great deal from this figure.

Their modern names are Cassiopeia A (Cas A) and Cygnus A (Cyg A).

"However, it is suggested that this disturbance is in some way connected with the amount of material in space."*

* Remember "Cygnus" and "amount of material in space"—they'll come up again.

Research slowed for a while around this time, as scientists and engineers turned their attention to inventing radar and other ways to end WWII...like the atomic bomb.

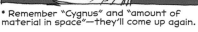

J. Robert Oppenheimer played a major role in that, but before the war he'd done important work in cosmology.

With Robert Serber and George Volkoff he'd studied neutron stars—the faster-spinning, more magnetic, and more massive cousins to white dwarfs.

OPPENHEIMER

SNYDER

VOLKOFF

SERBER

And with Hartland Snyder, he'd calculated that an imploding star can form a gravitationally collapsed object.

It shrinks to its Schwarzschild radius...and then might shrink even further.

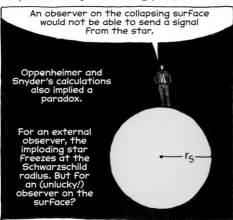

An observer on the collapsing surface would not be able to send a signal from the star.

Oppenheimer and Snyder's calculations also implied a paradox.

For an external observer, the imploding star freezes at the Schwarzschild radius. But for an (unlucky!) observer on the surface?

r_S

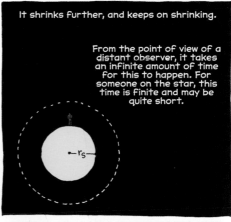

It shrinks further, and keeps on shrinking.

From the point of view of a distant observer, it takes an infinite amount of time for this to happen. For someone on the star, this time is finite and may be quite short.

r_S

For a Sunlike star, it would take about a day for it to close itself off from any communication with a distant observer—only its gravitational field would persist.

That idea that only the gravitational field would remain was just too...weird. So like Eddington and Einstein and so many before him, Oppenheimer backed off from calling it what it was.

A singularity.

But you can see where this is all heading.

Theorists were dancing around—and often backing away from—the idea of massive stars turning into singularities...

...while astronomers—like Martin Ryle at Cambridge—were building telescopes to pinpoint the origin of cosmic radio waves.

By then they knew how those radio waves formed: cosmic-ray electrons spiraling around interstellar magnetic fields.

The closest were in the center of the Milky Way—but they were strong enough to annoy people talking on the phone.

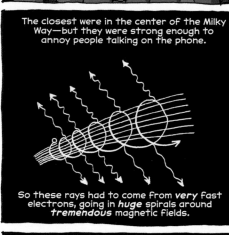

So these rays had to come from *very* fast electrons, going in *huge* spirals around *tremendous* magnetic fields.

It turns out that the only plausible source for all that energy, and the amazingly bright quasars also discovered at the time, couldn't be chemical...

...nuclear...

...or even matter/antimatter annihilation.

All that was left was gravity.

Gravity on a scale that had never been seen. Gravity from unimaginably massive objects.

"unimaginably massive objects"

"never been seen"

You're getting the picture. And astronomers and cosmologists were too.

John Wheeler got into the game at this point. He was skeptical of stellar implosions.

Wouldn't the simplest assumption be that such masses continually contract and ultimately cut themselves off from the universe?

It's very difficult to believe that "gravitational cutoff" is a satisfactory answer.

It *was* difficult, until David Finkelstein resolved Oppenheimer's paradox by creating a mathematical framework accommodating both an observer on an imploding star and one far away from it.

Wheeler eventually came around, with the zeal of a convert...

...a convert who had done the math, and had seen that it was good.

Have you heard the news?

He started working on the collapsed-star problem in earnest, and attracted a new group of students.*

JACOB BEKENSTEIN   DIETER BRILL   HUGH EVERETT   KIP THORNE   CHARLES MISNER

* Richard Feynman, his *other* famous student, had long since graduated and was busy doing other things.

They studied singularities and wormholes and whether there may be multiple universes.

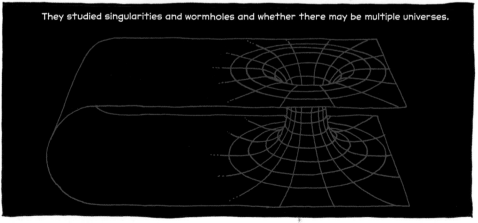

Golden Age (1963–1975)

And in 1963 Roy Kerr solved the Einstein field equations for a rotating star. Two years later, Ted Newman generalized Kerr's solution.

ROY KERR

TED NEWMAN

Now scientists could model charged, rotating, collapsed stars.

A golden age had begun, and the names of people investigating these crazy things started piling up...

In Russia, Igor Novikov and Yakov Zel'dovich proposed a way to search for collapsed stars.

IGOR NOVIKOV

Look for a frozen star dragging gases away from a visible companion star.

The gas particles* will collide on the opposite side of the frozen star, producing X-rays.

* Here on Earth, we call those gases from the Sun the solar wind.

And along with Andrei Doroshkevich, Novikov and Zel'dovich asked what an imploding star that wasn't perfectly spherical would turn into.

ANDREI DOROSHKEVICH

If the visible star is clearly orbiting something invisible, and you see the X-rays...*BOT!**

So the first thing to do is invent a good X-ray telescope.

Would you get a lumpy singularity?

* BOT = voilà!

All the while the arms race—a disturbing echo of World War II's big bang(s)—played in the background.

I was active in "Ban the Bomb" marches.

On the bright side, computing power and code written to create "better" atomic weapons was also useful for simulating stellar implosions.

The simulations confirmed that Oppenheimer and Snyder were right about collapsing stars.

Also, that you get the same singularity no matter what shape you start with.

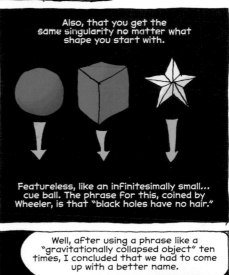

Featureless, like an infinitesimally small... cue ball. The phrase for this, coined by Wheeler, is that "black holes have no hair."

Black hole?

Well, after using a phrase like a "gravitationally collapsed object" ten times, I concluded that we had to come up with a better name.

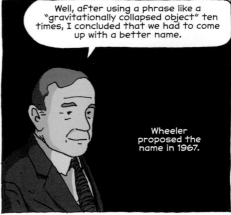

Wheeler proposed the name in 1967.

It caught on.

In England, George Ellis and I—along with Dennis's other students Martin Rees and Brandon Carter—were working on these problems at the start of the golden age.

Roger Penrose, at Oxford, was a major influence.

The discovery of the quasi-stellar radio sources has stimulated renewed interest in gravitational collapse.

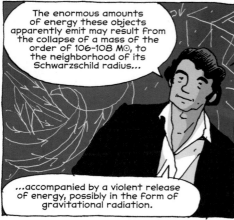

The enormous amounts of energy these objects apparently emit may result from the collapse of a mass of the order of 10^6–10^8 M⊙, to the neighborhood of its Schwarzschild radius...

...accompanied by a violent release of energy, possibly in the form of gravitational radiation.

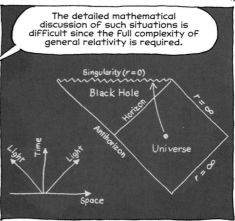

The detailed mathematical discussion of such situations is difficult since the full complexity of general relativity is required.

Singularity ($r = 0$)

Black Hole

Horizon

Antihorizon

$r = \infty$

$r = \infty$

Universe

Light

Time

Light

Space

Roger's initial results on this appeared around the time I was finishing my doctorate.

All done with the thesis, eh?

...

No, not yet. Listen to this:

"Full details of this and other related results will be given elsewhere."

You aren't thinking of concluding your dissertation *that way*, are you?

Hah. No. It's tempting, but no.

That's how Roger ends *his* paper! Rather bold to close with "To be continued."

Like a cliff-hanger at the end of a good science fiction yarn.

But much more exciting, because real science is actually happening out there.

Proving black holes were real was the challenge.

And now that I was married, another challenge—a paying job.

BRANDON CARTER
MARTIN REES

Tutoring undergraduates wasn't enough, so I applied for a research fellowship at Gonville and Caius College.

Dennis asked a famous steady-stater— Hoyle's colleague Hermann Bondi—to write me a letter of recommendation. I'd met him many times at King's College London.

HERMANN BONDI

We—Martin, George, Brandon, and I— were much more interested in what Roger was doing.

So I probably didn't make a big impression on Bondi.

I definitely didn't.

Ah...he apparently told them he's never heard of you.

Oh. Um.

That's... bad, isn't it?

I'll remind him—he'll write another recommendation.

Dennis did, and because of Bondi's embarrassment, his letter was probably far better than I deserved...

...and I got the fellowship. Not much pay, but not many responsibilities either.

I'd had the good sense not to ask for a recommendation from Hoyle, especially since I was writing a paper about the Hoyle-Narlikar theory...

...in which I pointed out some well-known problems.

No, I mean how 'bout, "One of the weaknesses of the Einstein theory of relativity is that although it furnishes field equations, it does not provide boundary conditions for them."

"Thus it does not give a unique model for the universe but allows a whole series of models."

"On the Hoyle-Narlikar Theory of Gravitation"
Proc. R. Soc. Lond. A vol. 286, no. 1406: 313–319. (1965)

...The paper also offered them a solution to the problem I'd pointed out at Hoyle's lecture.

"A possible way to save the Hoyle-Narlikar theory would be to allow masses of both positive and negative sign."

Nobody thought it was an *appealing* solution, though.

"The introduction of negative masses would probably raise more difficulties than it would solve."
...

"Probably"? Rather an understatement there, Stephen.

I suppose it is.

There was no evidence—there still isn't—that negative masses exist, after all.

So the difficulties faced by the steady-state theory were *large*.

It was an exciting time.

...rather tedious, yes. I leave for London early every Monday.

In class all week.

Then a dash for the tube on Friday evening and back on the train bound for Cambridge.

...We're in time for Pevsner's lecture this evening on Palladian villas.

Won't you come with me?

Not very interested in that.

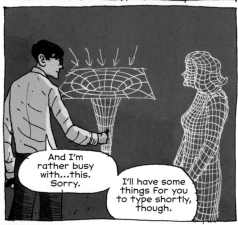

And I'm rather busy with...this. Sorry.

I'll have some things for you to type shortly, though.

Of course.

I'll be back in an hour or so. Longer if I attend services afterward.

Right. When did you say you'll be back?

A metaphor (1965)

She kept up her weekly commute between Cambridge and London for a year while finishing her baccalaureate degree in medieval literature.

I don't know that I demonstrated the appropriate interest at the time...

...very talented.

ALAN DREYERMUND, JANE'S UNDERGRADUATE ADVISOR

...though I did on occasion make the trip to London myself, of course.

I'm encouraging our Jane to pursue a PhD, in fact.

Well, it's a bit esoteric, isn't it?

I mean, studying medieval literature is about as useful as studying pebbles on a beach.

...

Perhaps, but didn't Newton himself say "I do not know what I may appear to the world..."

...but to myself I seem to have been only like a boy playing on the seashore, and diverting myself in now and then finding a smoother pebble or a prettier shell than ordinary...

111

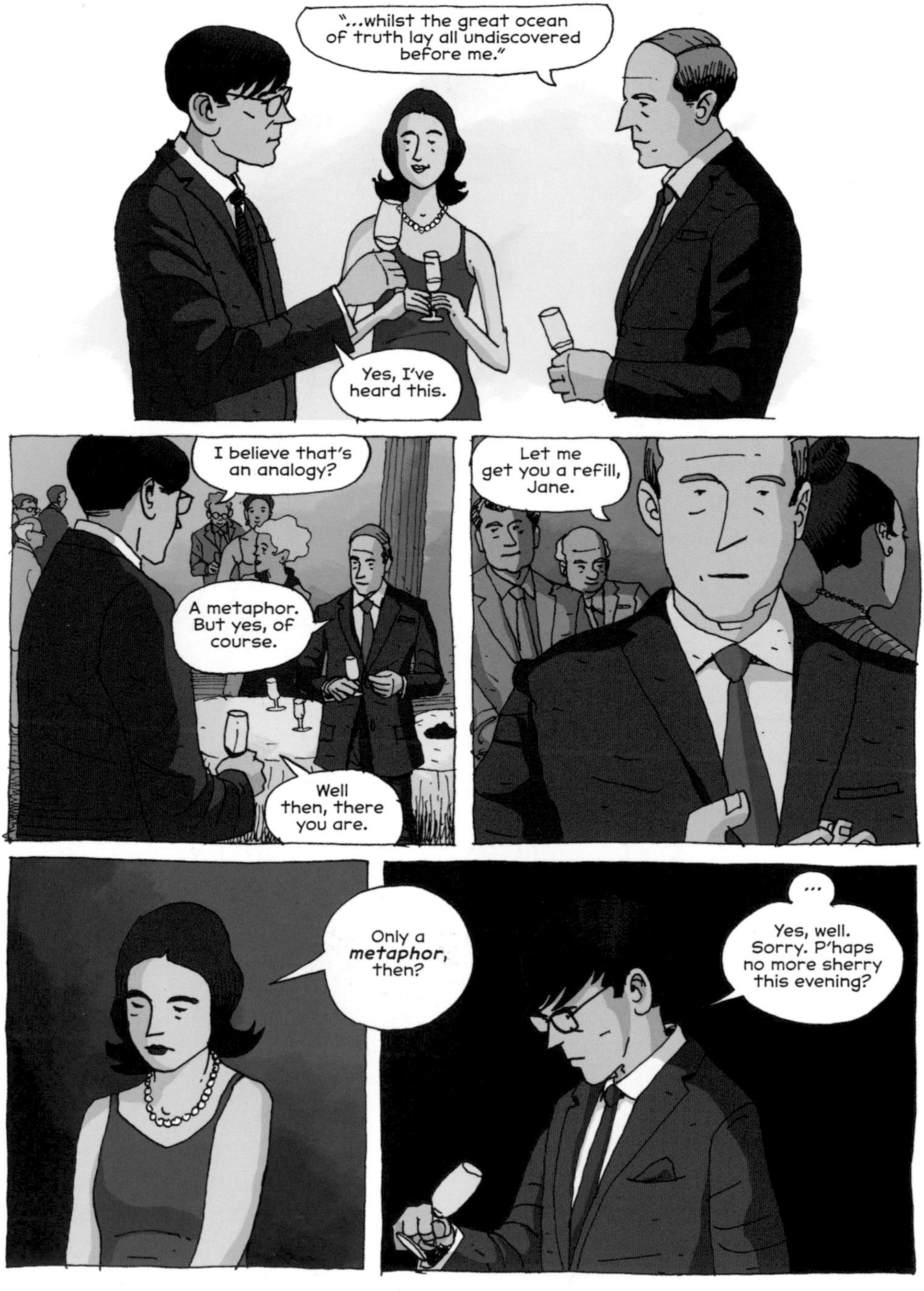
"...whilst the great ocean of truth lay all undiscovered before me."
Yes, I've heard this.
I believe that's an analogy?
A metaphor. But yes, of course.
Well then, there you are.
Let me get you a refill, Jane.
Only a *metaphor*, then?
...
Yes, well. Sorry. P'haps no more sherry this evening?

This routine lasted until Jane graduated.

We occasionally traveled together as well, of course.

Platform 3a

A week's honeymoon in Suffolk...

...followed by a summer school on general relativity at Cornell University.

The dormitory wasn't ideal for newlyweds, but many leading cosmologists were there.

We then went on to Miami Beach and a physics conference...

Physicists can look out of place almost anywhere, but this was a singular case.

I'm sorry. Would you mind saying that again?

What Stephen meant was...

So good to see you again, and so soon! How was the flight?

From there we went on to Austin, staying with George Ellis and his wife.

Where we did a bit of work, of course.

And then, back home.

Homes, really.

But by the time Jane graduated, we did have a more permanent residence, just a few doors down from the house we had rented.

Quite cozy, and convenient to my office at the Department of Applied Mathematics and Theoretical Physics.*

A normal life. Things to do, to look forward to.

It's the Thornes. Kip, Linda, do come in!

* DAMTP for short.

$$P = \frac{dE}{dt} = -\frac{32}{5}\frac{G^4}{c^5}\frac{(m_1 m_2)^2(m_1 + m_2)}{r^5}$$

The verse was written in Castilian— it was a time of transition.

I'm very tired so I'm *going* to bed.

But please, do stay.

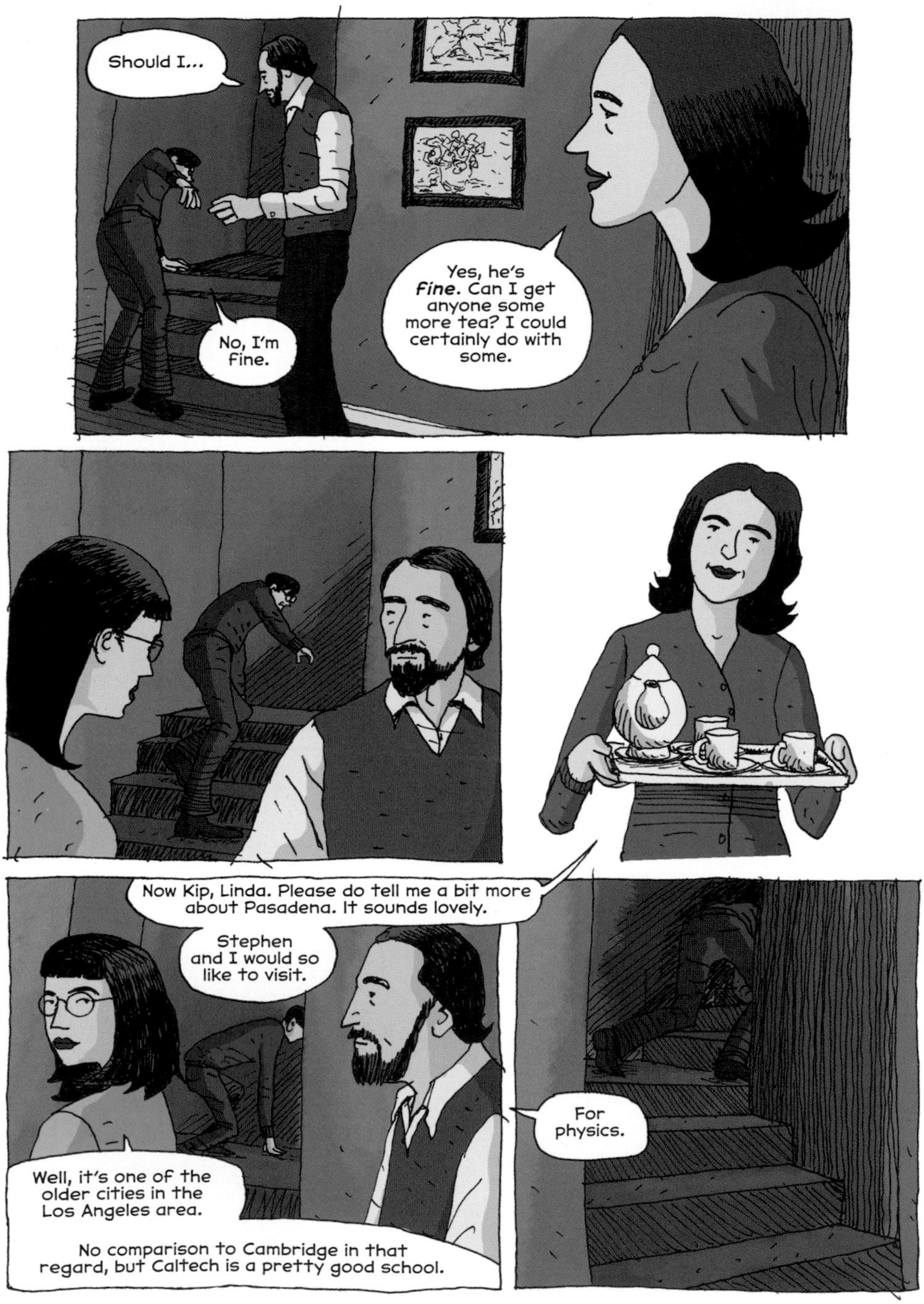
Should I...
No, I'm fine.
Yes, he's *fine*. Can I get anyone some more tea? I could certainly do with some.
Now Kip, Linda. Please do tell me a bit more about Pasadena. It sounds lovely.
Stephen and I would so like to visit.
Well, it's one of the older cities in the Los Angeles area.
No comparison to Cambridge in that regard, but Caltech is a pretty good school.
For physics.

"Singularities and the Geometry of Space-Time" (1966)

I wasn't the only winner that year, though. My essay tied with Roger's "An Analysis of the Structure of Space-Time."

"Recent work by Penrose (1965) and the author (1966)..."

Future collaboration between us was, perhaps, inevitable.

In his 1965 paper, Roger had suggested the following:

"After a certain critical condition has been fulfilled, deviations from spherical symmetry cannot prevent space-time singularities from arising."

Together, we posed this question:

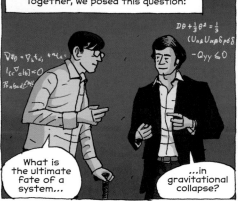

What is the ultimate fate of a system...

...in gravitational collapse?

Will a singularity in space-time ensue?

Or will asymmetries cause the different parts of the collapsing material to miss each other, leading to some *form* of *bounce*?

Five theorems and 18 pages of proof later, we showed that there is no bounce.

Meaning black holes really are all alike—they *don't* have hair.

Not that we said "black hole" or "hair," of course.

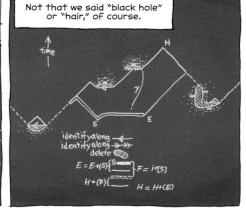

"The Singularities of Gravitational Collapse and Cosmology"
Proc. R. Soc. Lond. A vol. 314, no. 1519: 529–548. (w/ R. Penrose, 1970)

But we did say the following...

The instability of gravitation *presumably* results in regions of *enormously* large curvature in our universe.

These curvatures would have to be so large that our present concepts of local physics would become *drastically* modified.

And you'll see our theorems imply the existence of an initial "big bang"-type singularity at the beginning of the universe.

That depends on certain conditions being met that may well not apply to the *actual* universe.

Of course, those conditions are virtually unverifiable by observation.

Bondi submitted the paper to the Royal Society on our behalf, which was rather sporting of him, all things considered.

It was good work, and set me on a fruitful course.

"Drastically modified" physics, is it?

How might you accomplish that?

One...

One ought to look at the quantum aspects of gravitation.

"*One* ought to," is it?

...

Yes, well, I suppose I could.

I think you *should*.

And into the quicksand with you, then, my beamish boy.

It was an exciting time.

While we were working on these ideas, my son Robert was born.

Soon after we traveled to the Battelle Institute's summer school in Seattle...

...to Berkeley, California...

I'll be finished here at about 5 p.m. and...

No, you won't. But it's all right. I'll see you when you're done.

...and then to the University of Maryland to visit with Charles Misner, one of Wheeler's students.

Jane, you look...

I.

I'm all right. Perhaps it's just jet lag. I don't know, I...

I'm all right.

No, it's fine. I can manage.

Of course you are. Sit.

This is Robert? He's adorable!

Now, let me get you some coffee. Or would you rather tea?

Yes, of course.

The paper's in my bag. Jane, could you please lend a hand over here for a moment?

So many people to see.

It was quite productive.

The disease, on the other hand, continued its trajectory. Slower than anticipated, but inexorable.

My father had taken over my treatment—vitamins and steroids.

Effective, but even so, since the end of the 1960s my hands had taken on a permanent curl.

I could write my name, but that's all.

Stephen, we should really talk about—

'M doing fine. Don't need *outside* help, don't want a nurse.

And eventually canes weren't enough for outside the house.

My office was in DAMTP, and I was a member of Hoyle's new Institute of Astronomy by then.

Still didn't look through telescopes.

Theory is much more interesting— Roger's in particular.

His idea that every black hole must have a singularity inside had fascinating implications.

And his method of proof, which combined the mathematics of general relativity...

Roger? I've called about this theorem of yours.

Okay, so imagine the edges as surfaces and that they're connected. I know it's not the usual sort of thing, but—

...with geometrical methods and topology, revolutionized the field.

Yes, yes. I see.

And these techniques were useful to someone who could spend less and less time writing equations while studying black holes.

...If black holes were real, that is. At this point we were all betting on it.

What do you think about this possibility, then? Assume that a black hole exists there.

Somewhere in *our* galaxy.

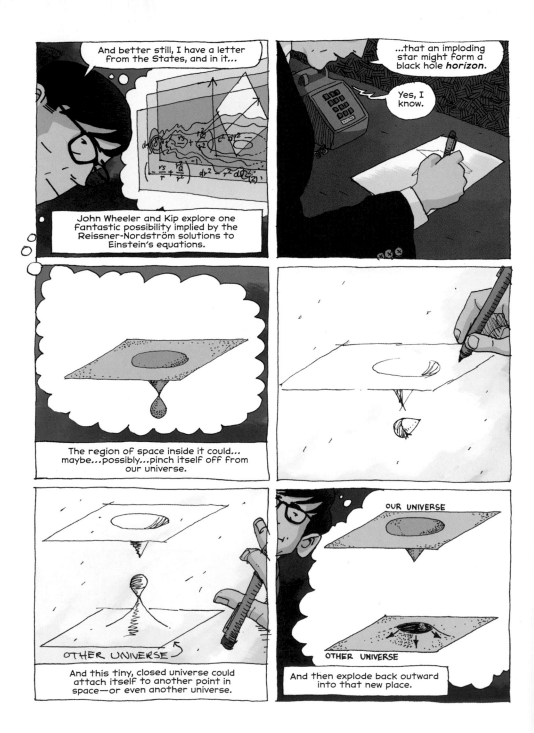

And better still, I have a letter from the States, and in it...

John Wheeler and Kip explore one fantastic possibility implied by the Reissner-Nordström solutions to Einstein's equations.

...that an imploding star might form a black hole *horizon*.

Yes, I know.

The region of space inside it could... maybe...possibly...pinch itself off from our universe.

And this tiny, closed universe could attach itself to another point in space—or even another universe.

OTHER UNIVERSE

OUR UNIVERSE

OTHER UNIVERSE

And then explode back outward into that new place.

Weird. Science-fictional. And as it turns out...

Do Kip and John really think this is possible? Because I think it's...

...unlikely.

Roger showed that any radiation that falls through such a horizon...

...and in our universe there will be plenty of radiation, since empty space ain't so empty...

...that radiation would destroy that pinched-off universe before it could go anywhere.

This hasn't stopped science fiction writers from adopting the idea, of course.

CONTACT
by
Carl Sagan

Years later Carl Sagan used it in the first draft of his novel *Contact*. But he wasn't up on the latest developments in this area.

Sagan was more concerned than most novelists with rigor, though, so he sent a draft of his book to Kip.

Kip caught the error and suggested he have the Ellie Arroway character travel via a wormhole instead.

...which is possible, at least in theory. Maybe.

Mm-hmm. Open wide, dear.

Roger also showed that a spinning singularity would drag the space-time in its neighborhood along with it.

Cosmic censorship (1969)

And if that wasn't enough, Roger also proposed the "cosmic censorship hypothesis."

Mm-hmm.

"Does there exist a 'cosmic censor' who forbids the appearance of naked singularities, clothing each one in an absolute event horizon?"

And then he references *my* work.

"In one sense, a 'cosmic censor' can be shown not to exist. For it follows from a theorem of Hawking that the 'big bang' singularity is, in principle, observable."

Of course, *no one* was there to observe the big bang.

No one.

I heard you the first time, dear. Are you suggesting a serious discussion of religion? You know I'd be glad of it...

And we both know what the other thinks, so what is there to discuss?

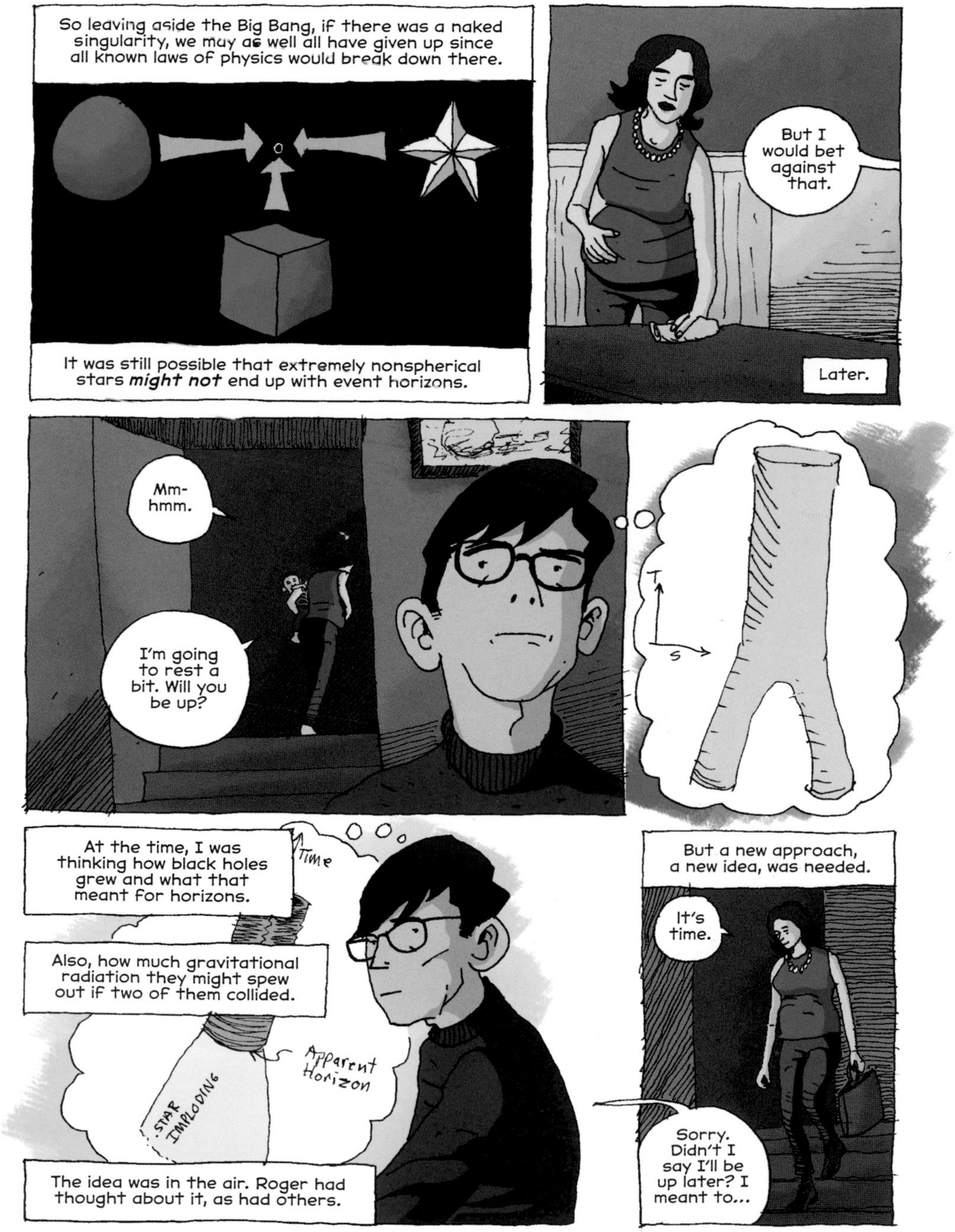
So leaving aside the Big Bang, if there was a naked singularity, we may as well all have given up since all known laws of physics would break down there.
It was still possible that extremely nonspherical stars *might not* end up with event horizons.
But I would bet against that.
Later.
Mm-hmm.
I'm going to rest a bit. Will you be up?
T
S
At the time, I was thinking how black holes grew and what that meant for horizons.
Time
Also, how much gravitational radiation they might spew out if two of them collided.
Apparent Horizon
STAR IMPLODING
The idea was in the air. Roger had thought about it, as had others.
But a new approach, a new idea, was needed.
It's time.
Sorry. Didn't I say I'll be up later? I meant to...

No.

Stephen.

It's time!

BANG!

Oh. Oh!

Roger had told me about conceiving the first of his singularity breakthroughs while crossing a street with a friend.

Then forgetting about it because they resumed their conversation...and later wondering why he felt so elated by the memory of something so ordinary as a walk.

It took him until late that night to remember that he'd figured out that a stellar implosion led to a black hole with a singularity inside.

His own "To be continued" idea.

When my breakthrough idea came, I was luckier in my circumstances.

Our daughter, Lucy, had just been born.

Bedtime story (1970)

Stephen, it's all right. Go on ahead and start getting ready for bed yourself.

Good night, my dear.

I'll just catch up on the bills downstairs.

Call me if...

I'll be fine.

Singularity
Light Ray Hits Singularity

Event Horizon

Interior of Black Hole

Light Ray Escapes

Distance from Singularity

Infalling Matter

Infalling Matter

Under the circumstances, can a black hole's event horizon ever shrink?

And what if two black holes collide? What would that look...

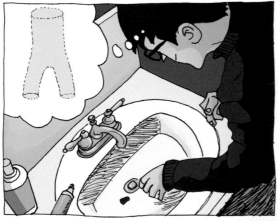

$$\text{Area}_1 \propto \text{Circumference}_1 \propto \text{Mass}_1^2$$
$$\text{Area}_2 \propto \text{Circumference}_2 \propto \text{Mass}_2^2$$
$$\text{but}$$
$$\text{Area}_{1+2} > \text{Area}_1 + \text{Area}_2 \Rightarrow \text{Mass}_{(1+2)}^2 > \text{Mass}_1^2 + \text{Mass}_2^2$$

The area must be larger, but what about...

CLICK

And gravitational-wave energy? How much...

This is reminiscent of the second law of...

Entropy.

What's that, dear?

$S = k \log W.$

I'm sorry, did you say something?

:sigh:

No, nothing.

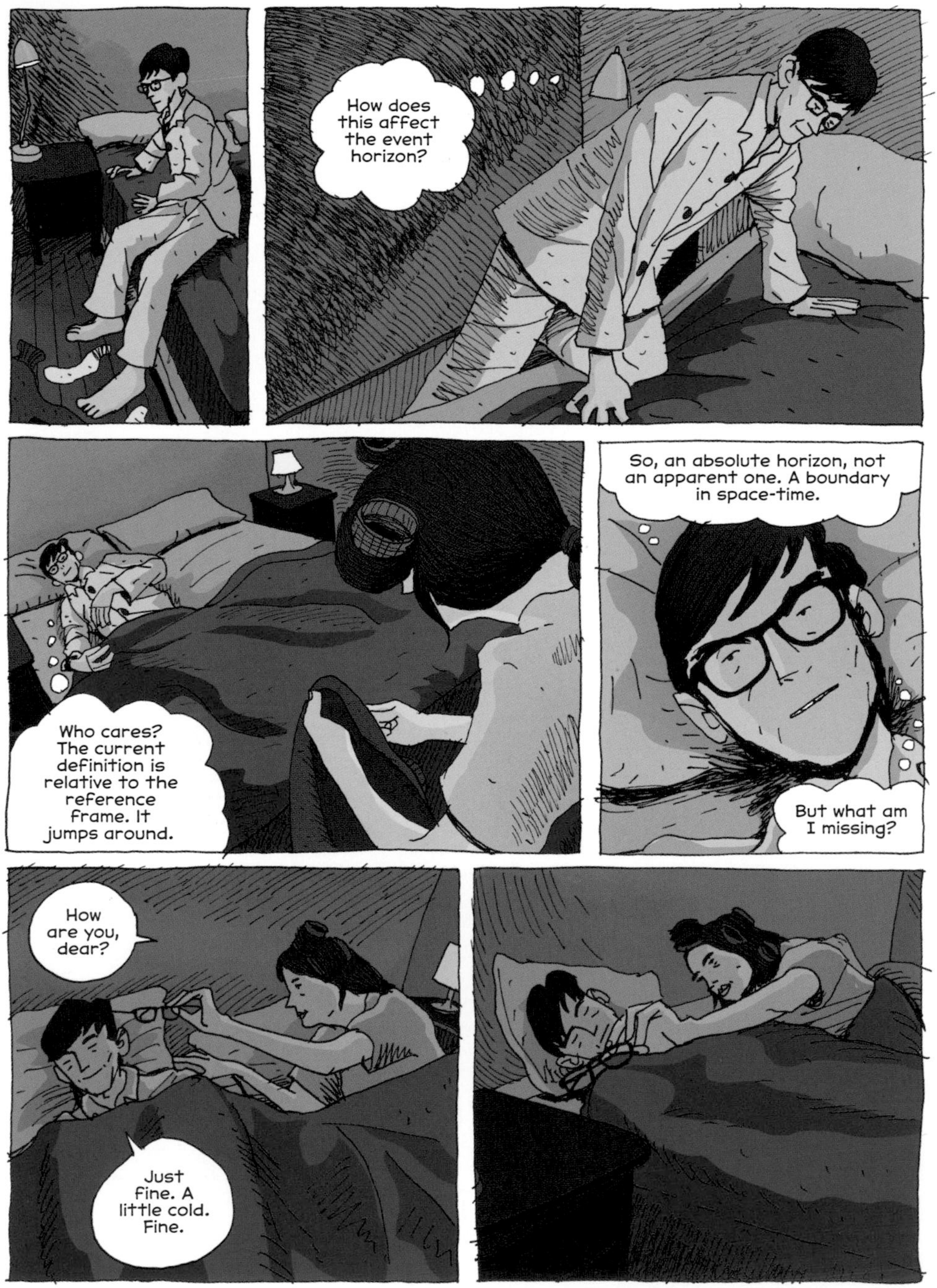
How does this affect the event horizon?
Who cares? The current definition is relative to the reference frame. It jumps around.
So, an absolute horizon, not an apparent one. A boundary in space-time.
But what am I missing?
How are you, dear?
Just fine. A little cold. Fine.

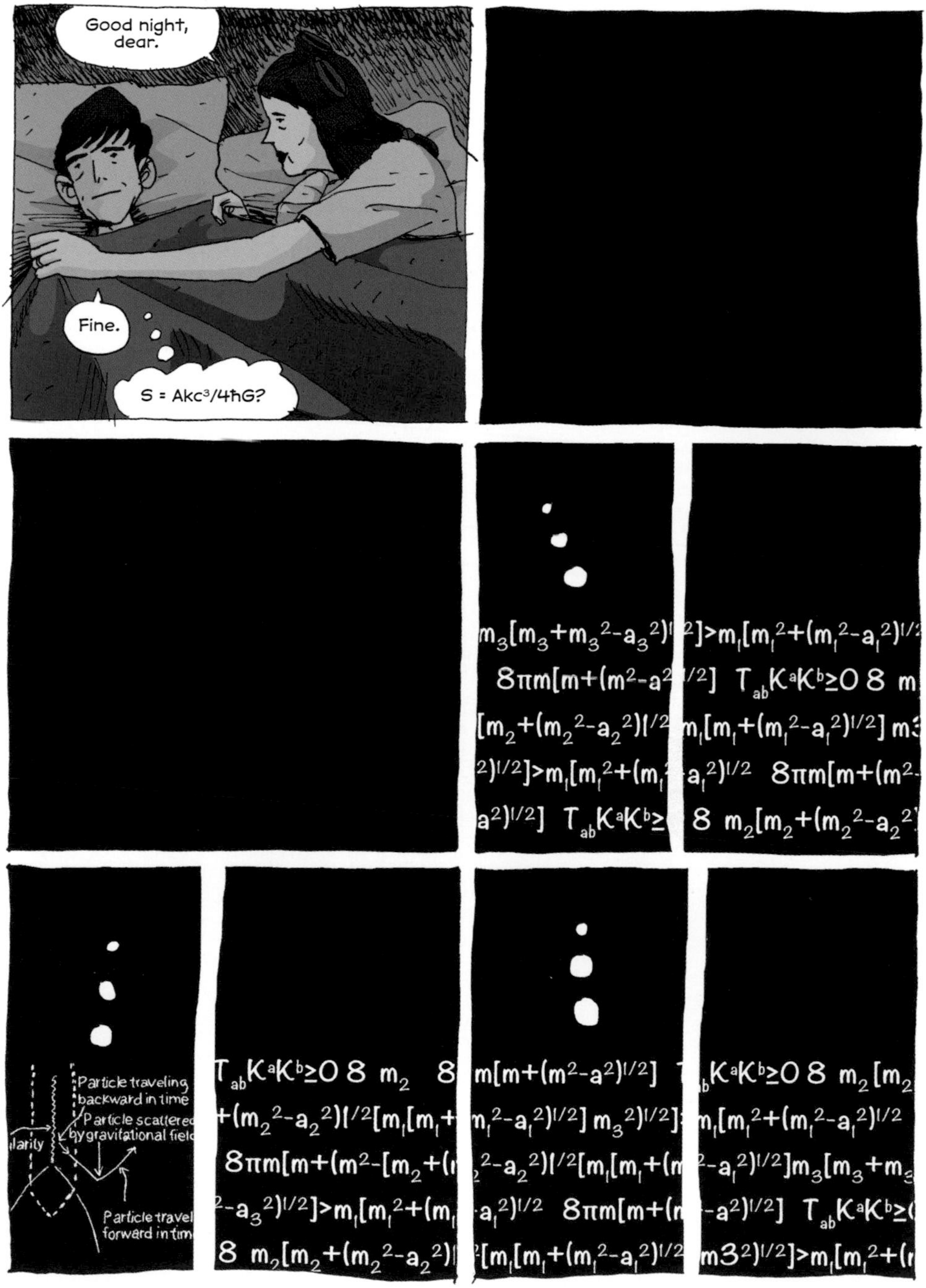
Good night, dear.
Fine.
S = Akc³/4ħG?
Particle traveling backward in time

I stayed awake as long as I could, so that even after sleep imposed a two-hour interruption...

...I remembered *exactly* why I was elated.

I'd seen that when two black holes collide, the area of the resulting event horizon must be *larger* than the sum of the two original horizons.

And I knew I could prove it.

I also knew the implications of this were profound.

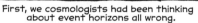

First, we cosmologists had been thinking about event horizons all wrong.

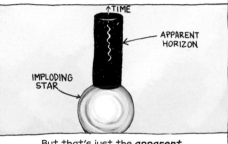

Until that night, we'd focused on the event horizon as the place where an observer sees that light is no longer escaping the black hole.

↑TIME

APPARENT HORIZON

IMPLODING STAR

But that's just the *apparent* horizon. It's there, but it may not look the same to everyone.

There's an *absolute* event horizon that is more fundamental and is the same for everyone, always.

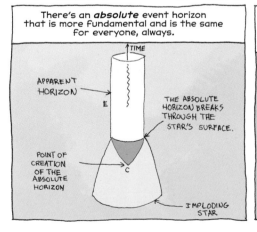

↑TIME

APPARENT HORIZON

E

THE ABSOLUTE HORIZON BREAKS THROUGH THE STAR'S SURFACE.

POINT OF CREATION OF THE ABSOLUTE HORIZON

C

IMPLODING STAR

That absolute horizon is where the collapsing star reaches the point of no return, and *future* signals from within won't make it out...

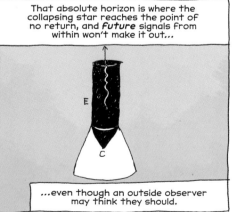

E

C

...even though an outside observer may think they should.

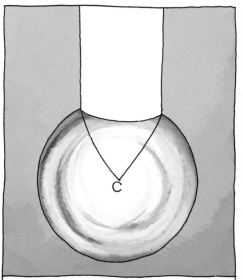

The absolute event horizon has two beautiful features. First, it doesn't abruptly change size or location. It's there, in the interior of a collapsing star, *before* an observer can see it.

As a star collapses and forms a black hole, the absolute event horizon grows.

When two black holes collide, it continues to grow.

And it grows in *anticipation* of matter falling in.

Yes, *anticipation*. Because that smooth increase stems from a third, surprising, feature...

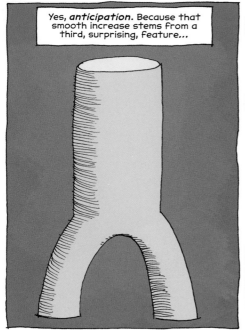

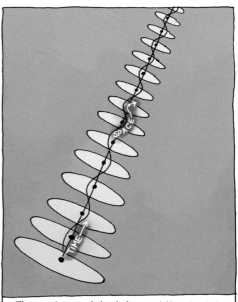

Time and space intertwine, and the absolute event horizon is the boundary for events that can send light out to an observer.

But photons are still escaping, which means the absolute event horizon starts growing *before* the matter that will make it grow gets swallowed.

...use and effect, reversed.

In effect.

You might find this hard to visualize.

It's certainly not *intuitive*, and most scientists didn't think such ideas were worth exploring.

No matter. Jim Hartle and I were able to calculate all the black hole properties I saw that night.

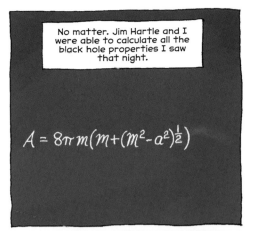

$$A = 8\pi m\left(m+(m^2-a^2)^{\frac{1}{2}}\right)$$

But that was just dotting the mathematical i's. I'd already crossed the theoretical t's.

$$\mu_{ab...d} = \lambda\,\mu^{(1)}{}_{ab...d}+O(\lambda^2)$$
$$T_{ab} = \lambda^2 T^{(2)}{}_{ab}+O(\lambda^3)$$

And they were beautiful.

As a result, my reputation grew.

$$\delta A = -\frac{4\pi}{\varepsilon^{(0)}}\exp(2\varepsilon^{(0)}t_0)\int \exp(-2\varepsilon\,{}^{(2)}{}_{ab}]^a\,d\Sigma^{l}$$
$$+ \frac{4\pi}{\varepsilon^{(0)}}\int T^{(2)}{}_{ab}]^a\,d\Sigma^{b}$$

JIM HARTLE

The topological and geometric methods that Roger had introduced to cosmology were perfect for certain kinds of problems.

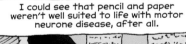

δA ... $\exp(2\varepsilon^{(}$

And those problems—the kind that could be approached visually—were perfect for me.

I could see that pencil and paper weren't well suited to life with motor neurone disease, after all.

We will reference the book I'm writing with George Ellis here, Jim.

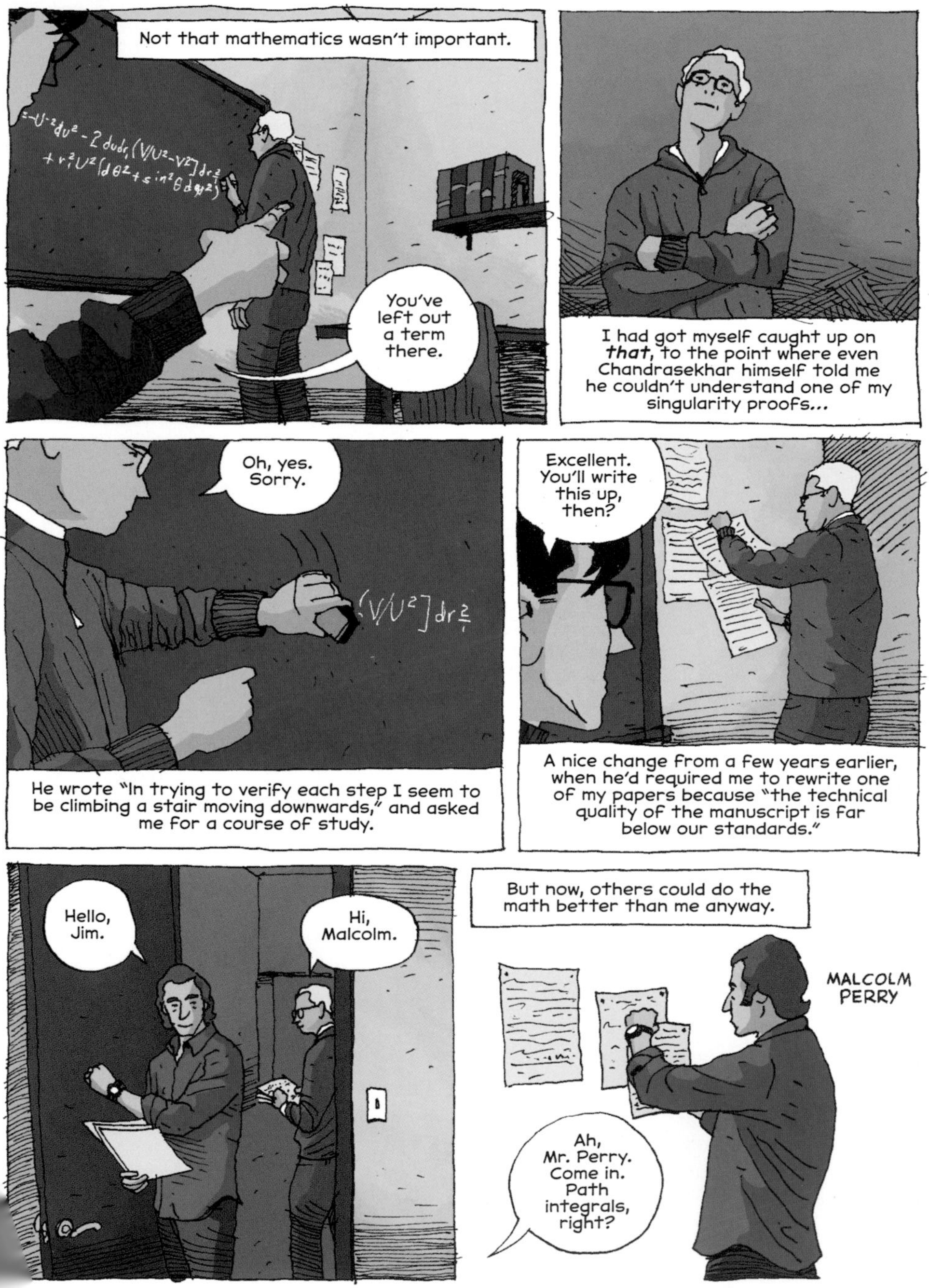
Not that mathematics wasn't important.
You've left out a term there.
I had got myself caught up on *that*, to the point where even Chandrasekhar himself told me he couldn't understand one of my singularity proofs...
Oh, yes. Sorry.
He wrote "In trying to verify each step I seem to be climbing a stair moving downwards," and asked me for a course of study.
Excellent. You'll write this up, then?
A nice change from a few years earlier, when he'd required me to rewrite one of my papers because "the technical quality of the manuscript is far below our standards."
Hello, Jim.
Hi, Malcolm.
But now, others could do the math better than me anyway.
MALCOLM PERRY
Ah, Mr. Perry. Come in. Path integrals, right?

The Large Scale Structure of Space-Time. (1973)

My first book, written with George Ellis, had a great deal of math in it, of course.

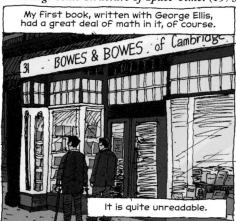

It is quite unreadable.

Except, perhaps, in the places we used Penrose diagrams.

These had become an essential tool for understanding black holes.

My understanding, at least.

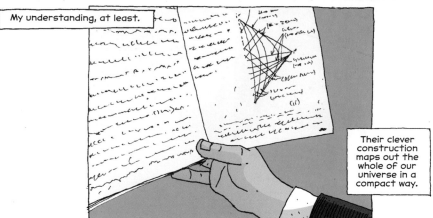

Their clever construction maps out the whole of our universe in a compact way.

In fact, they go beyond that.

They show space and time *inter-changing* at each event horizon.

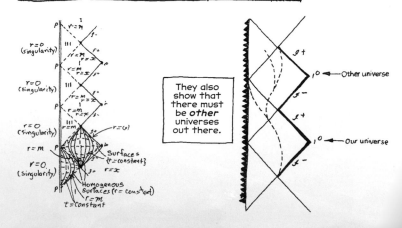

They also show that there must be *other* universes out there.

As a visual tool, they're essential.

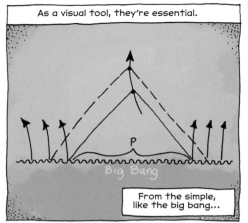

...to the more complicated, like Reissner and Nordström's spinning, charged holes.

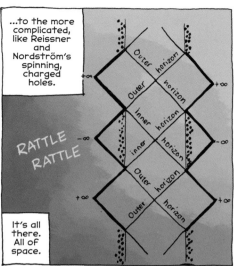

RATTLE RATTLE

It's all there. All of space.

From the simple, like the big bang...

Any amount of time.

Stephen.

Just washing up.

Stephen, it's late.

I'll be down shortly.

Not likely.

All right. Do hurry.

Most of my colleagues came around to my way of thinking about event horizons.

Some came around too far, though.

Wheeler's student Jacob Bekenstein, for instance.

Stephen, what are you thinking?

You're not dressed. We'll be late for church.

Oh. That. Go *on* without *me*.

Yes.

Of course.

Bekenstein looked at my area increase theorem...

...noticed a resemblance between equations describing black hole growth and those of classical thermodynamics...

...and concluded that black holes have entropy.

...entropy is a ...ure of the ...nness—or ...er—in a ... space.

But black holes are the most *uniform* things you can imagine.

They also take up no space at all.

So this notion of a black hole having entropy was *clearly* nonsense.

...Yes, once you change out of your church clothes, dear.

You missed a lovely service, Stephen. You would have liked the choir, at least.

Daddy, we all sang!

Yes. I'm sure.

Hello, what's this?

My dolly. She sang too. Why didn't you come?

Leave that, please, Lucy.

I've been thinking.

There's a surprise.

No, I mean about the summer. Would you like to go to the French Alps?

It will be a wonderful vacation for us.

Vacation?

For us?

Well, there's also a summer school I'd like to attend.

Brandon Carter, John Bardeen, and I set Bekenstein straight at a 1972 conference in Les Houches.

This notion of entropy with regard to a black hole?

The Four Laws of Black Hole Mechanics

It can be no more than a metaphor.

Or an analogy.

Not even that, *really, since* we all know *that* black holes don't radiate.

We wrote a paper on it later, dismissing the idea in a somewhat light tone.

Everyone left France convinced I was right.

Black Holes and Entropy

Everyone except Bekenstein.

And Wheeler.

By the way, Jacob...

Your idea is just crazy enough that it might be right.

And perhaps a few Russians, like Yakov Zel'dovich.

But you must come. And it's in Moscow—it will be a fascinating vacation for you.

Just us this time...not the children.

Kip and I visited Zel'dovich in Moscow the next year.

ALEXEI STAROBINSKY

I learned of his work, with Alexei Starobinsky, on marrying quantum mechanics and general relativity...

...and how their calculations indicated that spinning black holes *can* spew out particles.

VODKA

I didn't like the marriage these Russians arranged, though.

Surprise and annoyance (1973–1974)

So I worked out my own.

Is...
Stephen
all right?

What?

I mean, he
hasn't said
anything for
hours, and,
well...

...

Oh for
heaven's
sake.

He's fine.

Stephen.

Stop doing physics.

Mmm?

It took months.

As we closed in on the answer, I expected to find the radiation Zel'dovich and Starobinsky predicted for spinning black holes.

Bekenstein will use this to support his idea that black holes have...

But I was rather *annoyed* to find that even nonrotating black holes create and emit particles. I discussed this with my student Gary Gibbons.

Entropy. And I don't like it.

You all but sneered at it. But what does that matter? You must let people know.

I will. When Gary and I have refined our *approximations* and *done* the calculations.

That's an understatement.

But word got out that I'd "changed everything."

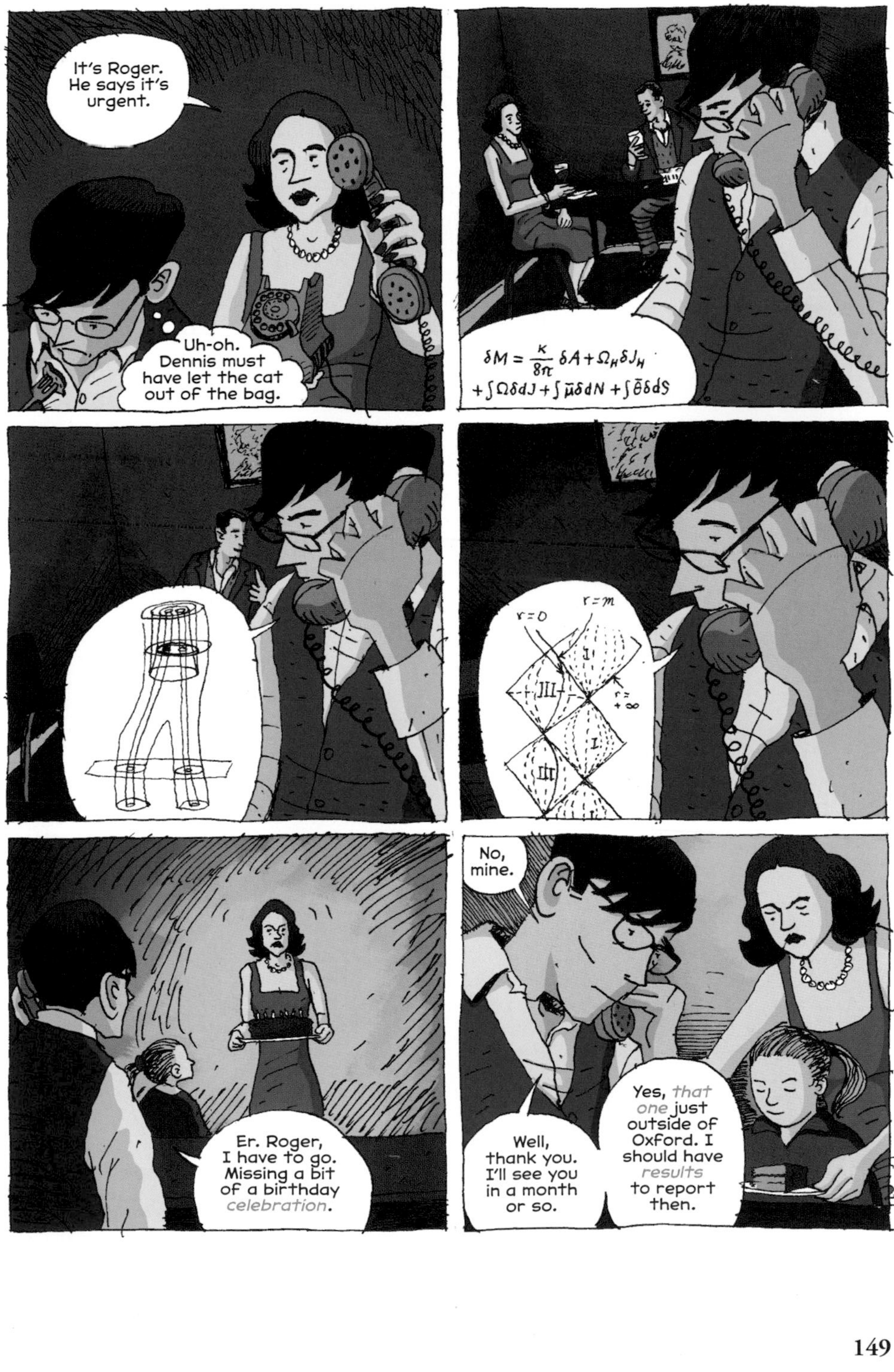
It's Roger. He says it's urgent.
Uh-oh. Dennis must have let the cat out of the bag.
$\delta M = \frac{\kappa}{8\pi}\delta A + \Omega_H \delta J_H + \int \Omega \delta J + \int \bar{\mu} \delta N + \int \bar{\theta} \delta S$
r = 0
r = m
r = +∞
No, mine.
Er. Roger, I have to go. Missing a bit of a birthday *celebration*.
Well, thank you. I'll see you in a month or so.
Yes, *that one* just outside of Oxford. I should have *results* to report then.

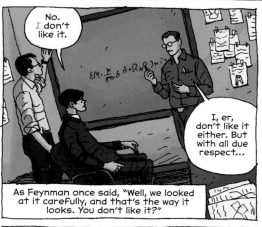

As Feynman once said, "Well, we looked at it carefully, and that's the way it looks. You don't like it?"

"Go somewhere else, to another universe where the rules are simpler—*philosophically* more *pleasing*."

We had found that all black holes emit radiation.

So I had to accept that Bekenstein was basically right about them having entropy.

I outlined my discovery at a conference in Oxford.

I Was Wrong

I began by...addressing... my previous position on Bekenstein's assertions about entropy.

I then went on to more interesting things—*why* I was wrong, and what that meant.

I described my hybrid approach to what happens at the event horizon of a black hole.

For *gravity*, I use the *classical theory* of general relativity.

As we know, black holes have an event horizon.

Per *Roger* Penrose, they prevent an *external* observer from being affected by the breakdown of predictability at singularities.

NO NAKED SINGULARITIES!

151

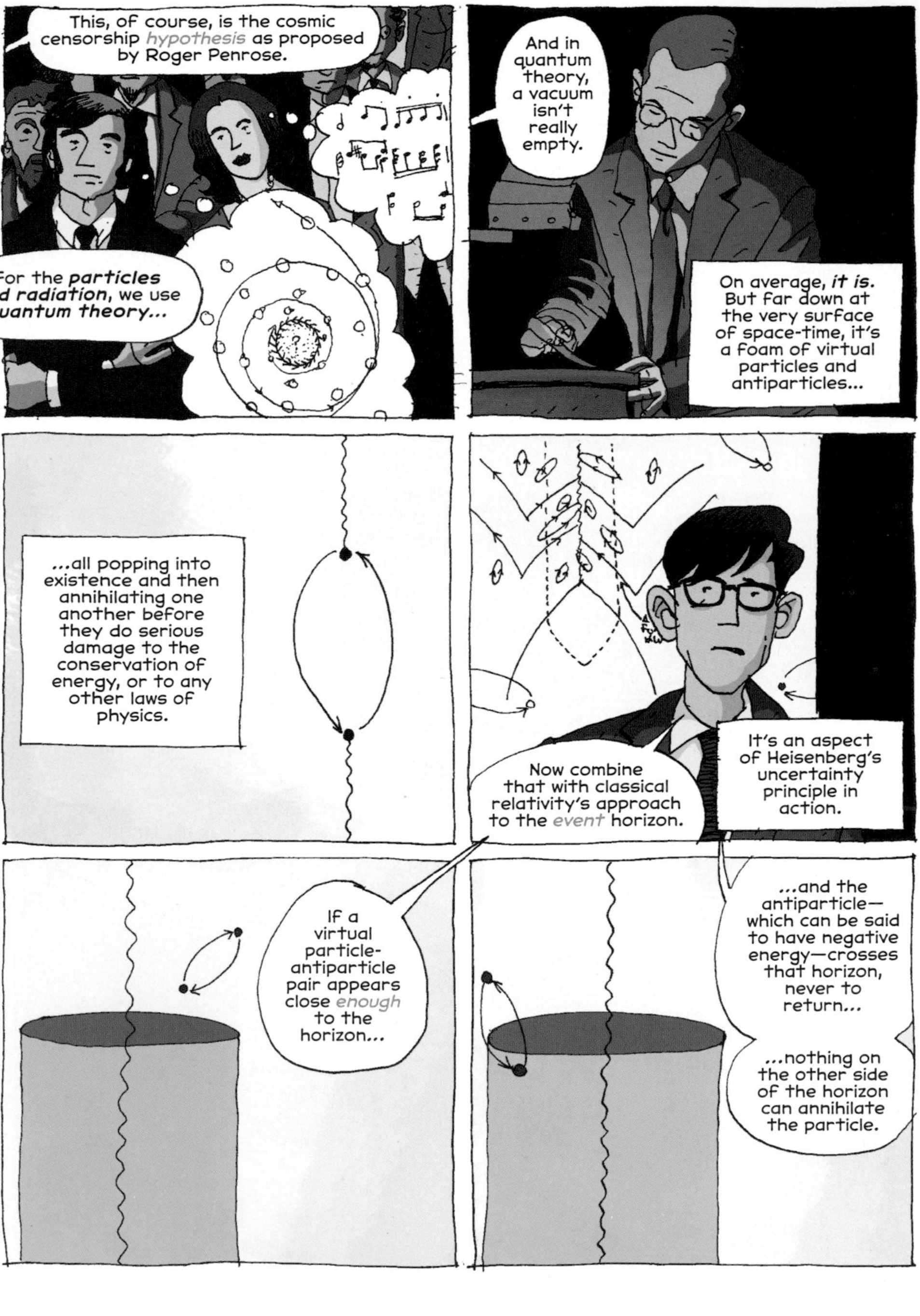
This, of course, is the cosmic censorship *hypothesis* as proposed by Roger Penrose.
For the ***particles and radiation***, we use ***quantum theory...***
And in quantum theory, a vacuum isn't really empty.
On average, ***it is.*** But far down at the very surface of space-time, it's a foam of virtual particles and antiparticles...
...all popping into existence and then annihilating one another before they do serious damage to the conservation of energy, or to any other laws of physics.
It's an aspect of Heisenberg's uncertainty principle in action.
Now combine that with classical relativity's approach to the *event* horizon.
If a virtual particle-antiparticle pair appears close *enough* to the horizon...
...and the antiparticle—which can be said to have negative energy—crosses that horizon, never to return...
...nothing on the other side of the horizon can annihilate the particle.

The antiparticle reduces the black hole's energy and is never seen again...

And the black hole, *in effect*, spews out the antiparticle's better half.

It radiates.

So in my union of quantum theory and classical relativity, a vacuum ain't empty, and...

...black holes ain't so black.

I don't think everyone understood. There weren't many questions, anyway, which is not a good sign.

And of course, the presentation was very technical and the arguments subtle and mathematical.

But that doesn't mean others didn't understand my conclusions. Or like them.

JOHN TAYLOR, SESSION MODERATOR

No more than I had liked Bekenstein's, to be fair.

I see there are no... I mean, no *more*, questions.

And for myself, I must say— negative-energy particles created right at the event horizon?

It was not the bombshell we thought it would be, I suppose.

I'm sorry, Stephen, but, this is absolute *rubbish*.

Let's move on to a paper by Dr. Isham...

"Black Hole Explosions?"
Nature vol. 248: 30–31. (1974)

I had already submitted a paper on it for publication.

"I would like to submit the enclosed paper 'Black hole explosions?' for publication in *Nature*."

"I realize that it is slightly long, but the result reported is rather sensational."

I sent it to *Nature*, probably the most prestigious scientific journal in the world.

"As rumors about my work have begun to spread, I feel that it is necessary to publish something as soon as possible."

Rumors? Does he think he's submitting to a tabloid?

"If you feel that the paper is too long for *Nature*, I would be grateful if you would return it so I can submit it elsewhere."

Too long?

"Yours faithfully," and so on.

"Yours,"

...

"Faithfully, S. W. Hawking."

Faithfully?

Just an expression.

Nature accepted the paper, published it in March, and even allowed the question mark to remain in the title.

I think you'll like this, Jacob. Hawking, expressing doubt!

Now people all over the world would know what I proposed.

"Bekenstein suggested on thermodynamic grounds that some multiple of the event horizon's area should be regarded as the entropy of a black hole."

I did more than *suggest* it!

"He did not, however, suggest that a black hole could emit particles as well as absorb them."

Of course I didn't. Nobody did, including *you*, Stephen.

Oh well...

156

"For this reason Bardeen, Carter, and I considered that the thermodynamical similarity between area and entropy was only an analogy."

"The present result seems to indicate, however, that there may be more to it than this."

I love that "only an analogy" bit. To dismiss it they write a ten-page paper with... 34 equations?

Methinks Hawking protests overmuch.

Black holes could evaporate and even explode if the conditions were just right.

This did *not* fit with dogma.

So scientists began to do what they do best. They looked for flaws in my theories...

...bad assumptions I might have made...

...and errors in my math.

Excellent.

Nothing we could find. But you should check it yourself.

Sounds good. I'm on my way to Moscow to meet with Zel'dovich and Starobinsky.

Anything specific we should look at?

The Russians were the last to come around.

⟨But...⟩

SCOTCH

⟨RUSSIAN⟩

⟨It will keep radiating, even after it stops spinning. Stephen has shown—⟩

Nyet, nyet, nyet. ⟨I have said all along—for years—the quantum field in curved space-time will **not behave** this way.⟩

⟨But... I... I'm sure Hawking is right.⟩

⟨I've shown you our work. All our assumptions. You tell me, where have my calculations gone wrong?⟩

⟨Well, if Stephen were here, I think he'd say...⟩

⟨Hah. I am asking *you.* So you and I, we agree, then, yes?⟩

158

Nyet, nyet, nyet.

But Kip was there when they did.

⟨Yakov Borisovich, my flight home leaves in just...⟩

⟨No. I mean, yes!⟩

⟨No, of course I want to talk, but I don't have enough time to pack and get to the airport as it is...⟩

⟨Yes, yes, I'll come over right now.⟩

Though just barely.

⟨We kept working after you left, and...⟩

⟨W-w-we give up!⟩

⟨Our calculations were wrong. Bad assumptions too.⟩

‹We were wrong!›

‹Now. We toast Hawking!›

Kip told us the good news when he got back home.

We were already in Pasadena for a sabbatical at Caltech.

...calling your partial marriage of general relativity and quantum theory "the laws of quantum fields in curved space-time."

Laws. *That's* good.

The Royal Society won't regret *inducting* me, then.

Ooh. Yesyesyes. Daddy says he got to write his name in a *big* book.

Did he, now? That's great.

The ceremony had taken place earlier that year, and was one of the last times I signed—or could sign—anything. I couldn't go to the book, so they brought it to me and I did it.

Some formalities must be observed, after all.

The only problem with my laws—or any of the laws about black holes—was that there were no experiments backing any of it up.

In fact, nobody had observed a black hole.

Not surprising, perhaps—being black and all—but still, that shouldn't have stopped us. Wheeler had described how to do it, in general terms.

Picture a dimly lit ballroom full of dancing couples.

All the women wear white gowns, and most of the men wear white tuxedos.

But a few of the men wear black.

But as we observe the women waltzing... orbiting...

We can be certain they have partners, even though we can't see all of them.

That was the situation with black holes. We suspected they were there, but had no direct observations.

I can write my name too. Would you like to see?

I *would!*

Later, dear. Let Daddy and Kip catch up.

Radio astronomers had identified some possibilities, but that's all they were. Possibilities.

Cygnus X-1 was one.

Cygnus

Kip and I had constant arguments about it.

WHIRRRZZZZZZ

So you're serious about this?

Yes. I don't like to live dangerously.

BAR

WHIRRRZZZZ

Okay then. Let's get some witnesses.

WHIRRRZZZZZ

DON PAGE

Whereas Stephen Hawking has such a large investment in general relativity and black holes and desires an insurance policy...

ANNA ZYTKOW

And whereas Kip Thorne likes to live dangerously without an insurance policy.

Therefore be it resolved...

I bet a one-year subscription to *Penthouse* for Kip against a four-year subscription to *Private Eye* for me that Cygnus X-1 did not contain a black hole above the Chandrasekhar limit.

I'd done a lot of work on black holes, and it would all be wasted if it turned out they didn't exist.

Why *Private Eye*? It's a bit...

I'll catch up with you later. Have to get this framed, I think!

In that case I would at least have the consolation of winning my bet.

⸬cough⸬

Satirical. And would *you* rather the *other*?

Good heavens, no.

163

In addition to black hole problems, I was now also working on the big bang and the origins of the universe.

And experiments were starting to catch up with theory.

Unlike strong radio waves from very specific locations—the hints of black holes that radio astronomers like Reber had found...

...astronomers Penzias and Wilson had recently discovered a uniform hiss that seemed to come from everywhere and nowhere.

...this *theory* conflicts with observation.

I must say, I still hear a little bit of that hiss.

Sorry, Professor Hoyle, let me make some adjustments.

That hiss is the *cosmic microwave background*. On your radio, you hear it as some of the noise between stations.

This can *hardly* be ignored.

It's the voice of the big bang, echoing through all of space-time.

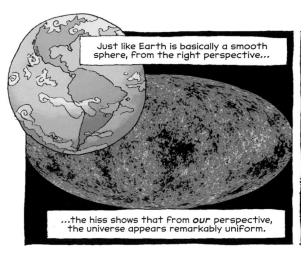

Just like Earth is basically a smooth sphere, from the right perspective...

...the hiss shows that from *our* perspective, the universe appears remarkably uniform.

The question is, why?

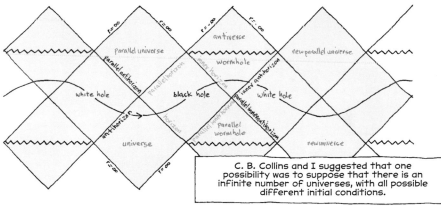

antiverse

parallel universe

new parallel universe

r = ∞

r = ∞

r = ∞

r = ∞

wormhole

parallel antihorizon

inner horizon

parallel horizon

inner antihorizon

white hole

black hole

white hole

antihorizon

parallel inner antihorizon

horizon

parallel inner horizon

parallel wormhole

universe

new universe

r = ∞

r = ∞

C. B. Collins and I suggested that one possibility was to suppose that there is an infinite number of universes, with all possible different initial conditions.

Only universes that *expand* at just *the* right speed would contain galaxies, and hence intelligent life.

The balance between large-scale uniformity and the right smaller-scale variations—from star systems to planets to people—is a delicate *one*.

So the fact that *we* observe the universe to be isotropic—uniform at *just the* right scale—would be simply a reflection of our own existence.

Anna! Any progress?

165

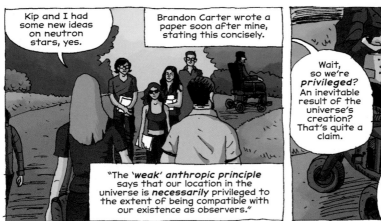

Kip and I had some new ideas on neutron stars, yes.

Brandon Carter wrote a paper soon after mine, stating this concisely.

Wait, so we're *privileged*? An inevitable result of the universe's creation? That's quite a claim.

"The *'weak' anthropic principle* says that our location in the universe is *necessarily* privileged to the extent of being compatible with our existence as observers."

Any more remarkable than the more... *common*...claims about *how the* universe began?

Perhaps you'll like *Carter's* **"strong" anthropic principle** better.

It states that *our* universe *must be such as* to admit the creation of observers within *it*.

We are here, so *the laws* of physics *must* be compatible with our existence. There *might be* other universes with different laws...

...but there won't—couldn't!— be anybody there to study them.

166

That's...

That's an interesting position to take, for a scientist.

Is it physics or, um, well... philosophy?

I suppose my work on the origin of the universe *is on the* borderline between science *and* religion.

But I try to stay on the scientific side of *that* border.

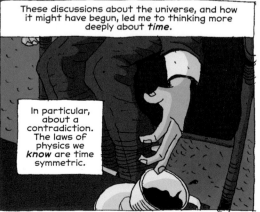

These discussions about the universe, and how it might have begun, led me to thinking more deeply about *time*.

In particular, about a contradiction. The laws of physics we *know* are time symmetric.

So they work the same if we run things forward or backward in time.

But the universe we live in certainly doesn't behave that way.

Entropy *always* increases with time.

Sorry.

Oh bother.

We never see it go the other way.

That's the thermodynamic arrow of time.

There's a psychological arrow as well—we remember events in the past.

But not the future.

And there's a cosmological arrow—the direction in which the universe is expanding.

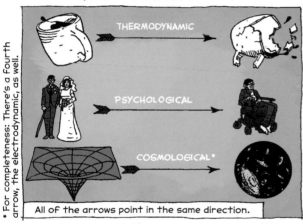

THERMODYNAMIC

PSYCHOLOGICAL

COSMOLOGICAL*

All of the arrows point in the same direction.

* For completeness: There's a fourth arrow, the electrodynamic, as well.

$\phi_0) = 0$

The question is why.

And you're predicting that the arrows should reverse in a **recontracting** phase of the universe?

I think you're going to have to wait a **long** time for the collapse of the universe.

Or *you could* jump into a black hole.

‹cough›

But then you would not be able to tell anyone *outside* whether I am right.

169

Furthermore, if the *thermodynamic* arrow **did** reverse, you would not remember jumping...

...because it would now be in your **future** rather than in the past.

I don't think you're going to be able come up with enough math to **prove** anything about this.

Perhaps *not.*

WHIRRRZZZ

But I'd rather be right than rigorous.

The God Hypothesis (1975)

Actually, I said that to Kip a few years later.

And the paper I wrote had quite a lot of math in it, as it turns out.

So much for "no rigor."

Don Page's analysis of the ideas, which appeared right after mine, didn't. It also contradicted some of my main findings.

Just before it was published I added a note to my paper saying I thought Don was right.

Mostly.

We moved soon after returning from Caltech, and Don came to live with us not long after that.

He and I worked together, of course, and he helped with some of my more mundane, daily needs as well.

Undergraduates lived above us. They had previously occupied the whole house, so there were a *lot* of things that needed fixing.

171

We partitioned off the stairs—I could no longer manage them—and took up residence on the ground floor.

Good morning. Sleep well?

Still a little jet-lagged, but yes. Fine. Thank you.

I'm an early riser anyway.

That's good, then. Let me show you the routine.

He'll take these pills with breakfast, along with a laxative.

That's quite...

A lot, yes. Stephen has taken to being his own doctor. I spend a fair amount of time at the chemist's.

So for food, it's boiled eggs, pork chops, rice, and tea. No toast for him, since that has gluten.

And I see you have the *Times*. Set it up on that stand.

He didn't seem to take much notice of the news in California, so why...?

Right. You haven't been to High Table yet.

He keeps up here so he'll have something to talk about with the other fellows at lunch.

We settled into a new routine fairly quickly.

Robert, you help Lucy, please. I'll go get your father.

Don, help yourself to some food.

We've cornflakes, muesli, toast. And I can make a boiled egg for you as well.

Good morning.

Good morning, Daddy.

Good morning, Daddy.

Good morning, Stephen.

You know, I was reading something interesting this morning.

It's from Hebrews 11:3— "Through faith we understand that the worlds were framed by the word of God, so that things which are seen were not made of things which do appear."

Prophetic, don't you think? Our world, the world that is seen, is made of things that do not appear. Elementary particles, in other words.

173

You really ought to consider—

Don, before you go on, wouldn't you like more toast?

I'm sorry. What?

Well. Um. Yes, I suppose. Thank you.

÷cough÷

And have you tried the Marmite yet?

No, I don't think we have this in the US.

It looks like it's some kind of chocolate, maybe?

Try it and see.

Oh my G...

...

Why would you...?

No more of that, yes?

Yes.

I... I'll clear away the dishes.

Thank you. And Robert, get yourself ready for school.

If you can help Lucy get ready too, maybe Daddy will read you a story before bed tonight.

Yes, I will. *Paddington Bears.*

Thank you. I *would have* thought you'd—

I'd what... *not* save you from it? I'm sure he knows you and I don't see eye to eye on this. But there's a time and a place for such things.

And the breakfast table is neither.

Pardon?

Nothing, Don. Just helping Stephen with his breakfast.

Though we disagreed about "such things," we understood each other.

And I wasn't completely averse to **everything** having to do with what Laplace called the "God hypothesis."

Not long before this, I was invited to Rome to receive the Pope Pius XII medal.

...giovane scienziato per un lavoro distinto.

...young scientist for distinguished work.

Thank you.

Thank you.

The Catholic Church liked the big bang theory, and my work on it, not only because of the Lemaître connection, but because it was compatible with doctrine.

Current doctrine, anyway.

I would like to see the Galileo documents.

Stephen asked if he could please now see the documents Galileo signed when he was... asked to recant.

Naturalmente. Il mio assistente li avrà pronti per te entro questo pomeriggio.

Of course. An aide will have them ready for you this afternoon.

350 years. Will there be an apology for the Church's *mistake*?

And...

No, Stephen.

Please.

And he suggests a formal apology for this might be in order.

Now that more than three centuries have passed.

...

I'm very sorry.

Non importa figliola, capisco. Prima che tu vada, posso benedirti?

Do not apologize, my child. I understand. Before you go, may I give you a blessing?

:cough cough:

We got different things out of the visit, I think.

Jane's religious convictions had been growing steadily stronger, so she liked meeting the Pope.

But as she said later, she had also grown tired of reflected honors.

Another medal. It's quite an honor, Ruth, and I really am terribly proud...

That sounds to me like "terribly proud *but...*"

Which is understandable.

It looks like you could do with a refill. I'll go boil—

I'm fine, dear. Sit. Please!

The no-boundary proposal (1975–1983)

And...if I may presume...

I thought you deserved to be given something too.

I returned to the Vatican in 1981, with a larger group.

It was for a scientific conference, not medals, and there I introduced the no-boundary proposal that Jim Hartle and I had developed.

It addressed the breakdown of *physics* at the big bang singularity, though the paper we wrote phrased it more modestly as the "breakdown of *predictability*."

So the boundary conditions of the universe are that it has no boundary. The universe wraps around itself in space-time.

I don't think the new Pope followed the conference closely.

He probably wouldn't have understood the quantum mechanical arguments, or the notion of imaginary time very well anyway.

And had he understood, he would **not** have liked the implications of my no-boundary ideas.

After all, in an eternal universe, what need for a creator?

He would have liked my principle of ignorance better.

The principle of ignorance (1975–1980)

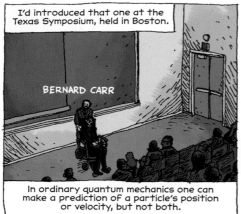

I'd introduced that one at the Texas Symposium, held in Boston.

BERNARD CARR

In ordinary quantum mechanics one can make a prediction of a particle's position or velocity, but not both.

The unpredictability of radiation from black holes is above and beyond that.

TIME

SPACE

In the case of particles emitted by a black hole, one cannot make any definite predictions at all.

Call it the "principle of ignorance."

Call it the "principle of ignorance."

This *inability* to know *either* a particle's position or velocity allowed me to expand on Einstein's famous quote about God.

God *not only plays dice, he sometimes throws* them *where they* can't *be* seen.

It's fun to make jokes at the expense of Einstein, but it was getting harder to make jokes of *any* kind.

God *not only* plays dice, he *sometimes throws them where they can't* be seen.

‑cough‑

By this time only my closest friends and family could understand me.

God not *only plays dice*, he sometimes throws *them where they* can't *be seen*.

Oh. Oh! Hah... I got it.

God not only plays dice, he sometimes throws them where they can't be seen.

HAH!

HA HA!

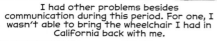

I had other problems besides communication during this period. For one, I wasn't able to bring the wheelchair I had in California back with me.

CLAP CLAP CLAP CLAP

We petitioned the Department of Health to get one.

Out of the question.

They cite the expense, and how it isn't...essential?

It *is* quite expensive. I've totted it up, and it would take just about all our savings.

Well then, I suppose *for* now *we* cannot—

We'll do it.

We couldn't bring Pasadena's curb ramps back with us either.

Jane and I started petitioning the city for changes along those lines as well.

I wrote many letters.

"The areas where dropped curbs would be most useful are as follows: Senate House Hill, Robinson College," etc.

These met with success...

...eventually.

It helped that Gonville and Caius gave me a readership—so I at last had an official position at Cambridge.

÷cough cough÷

In addition to a ramp, I got a secretary—Judy Fella.

Good morning, Stephen.

Good morning.

Who's first, *then*?

All right.

Stephen, why don't I fill you in on where everyone is?

I'll start with me.

With the new position came graduate students. Malcolm had been my first, and since then had helped direct another one while I was in California.

...finishing up the paper on instabilities in gravity and supergravity.

Good. *Have* you read *Michio* Kaku's paper? I have it here.

I'm sorry, could you say that again?

Like most of my students—the ones who succeeded, anyway—he rather quickly became independent.

∹cough cough∹

I liked that he wasn't any trouble.

Oh wait. Kaku, right?

No, I've not seen it. This is for the *Superspace and Supergravity* volume?

I was editing a book with contributors from all over the world.

Sorry, equation 15 here has a mistake. Judy, could you please...?

I wanted a color cover.

How about that area over *to the* left?

Over there, I think.

Cambridge University Press said it wasn't worth the expense.

I'm afraid it simply won't increase sales for a book of *this* type.

∹cough∹

I threatened to withdraw the manuscript, so they relented. But sales did not in fact meet expectations.

185

Before that, I'd edited *General Relativity: An Einstein Centenary Survey*, also for Cambridge University Press. It sold well—and later won the Einstein medal.

We also had another son, Timothy, and Jane completed her thesis on medieval Spanish poetry.

Our hands were full, and having drained our savings to buy the chair—and some independence—money was tight.

School bills were mounting as well, so I began to think about writing another book.

One that might *sell*, regardless of the cover.

There were many possible subjects.

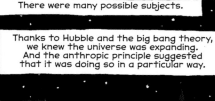

Thanks to Hubble and the big bang theory, we knew the universe was expanding. And the anthropic principle suggested that it was doing so in a particular way.

A way that is well tuned to produce just the right kind of lumpiness in the fabric of space-time to allow for stars to clump into galaxies...

...matter to clump into stars...

...and stardust to clump into physicists.

Fatal flaws (1981–1982)

We met in Moscow to talk about this.

I presented a paper on the inflation of the universe and the problems with prevailing theories attempting to explain it.

It was a difficult talk to give—I had not prepared the text in advance, so it had to be translated into Russian on the fly.

I begin with **Guth's** *proposals.*

I...will start by discussing the theories of Guth.

Andrei Linde did the translating. Word-for-word, at first.

⟨First, the theories of Guth.⟩

The problems *with the older* inflation *model are as follows...*

The problems with...

⟨The problems with Guth's model are as follows.⟩

First, the Higgs *Field question.*

The... Higgs field.

¡cough cough¿

⟨Russian⟩

...

Ah, I see where this is going.

ooo

⟨The symmetry problems and their almost instantaneous disruption of the Higgs field are the first of many difficulties.⟩

Linde knew the area well, and elaborated on some of my explanations.

This worked well, especially when I began discussing his own theories.

Linde *has suggested an* interesting *solution to these problems.*

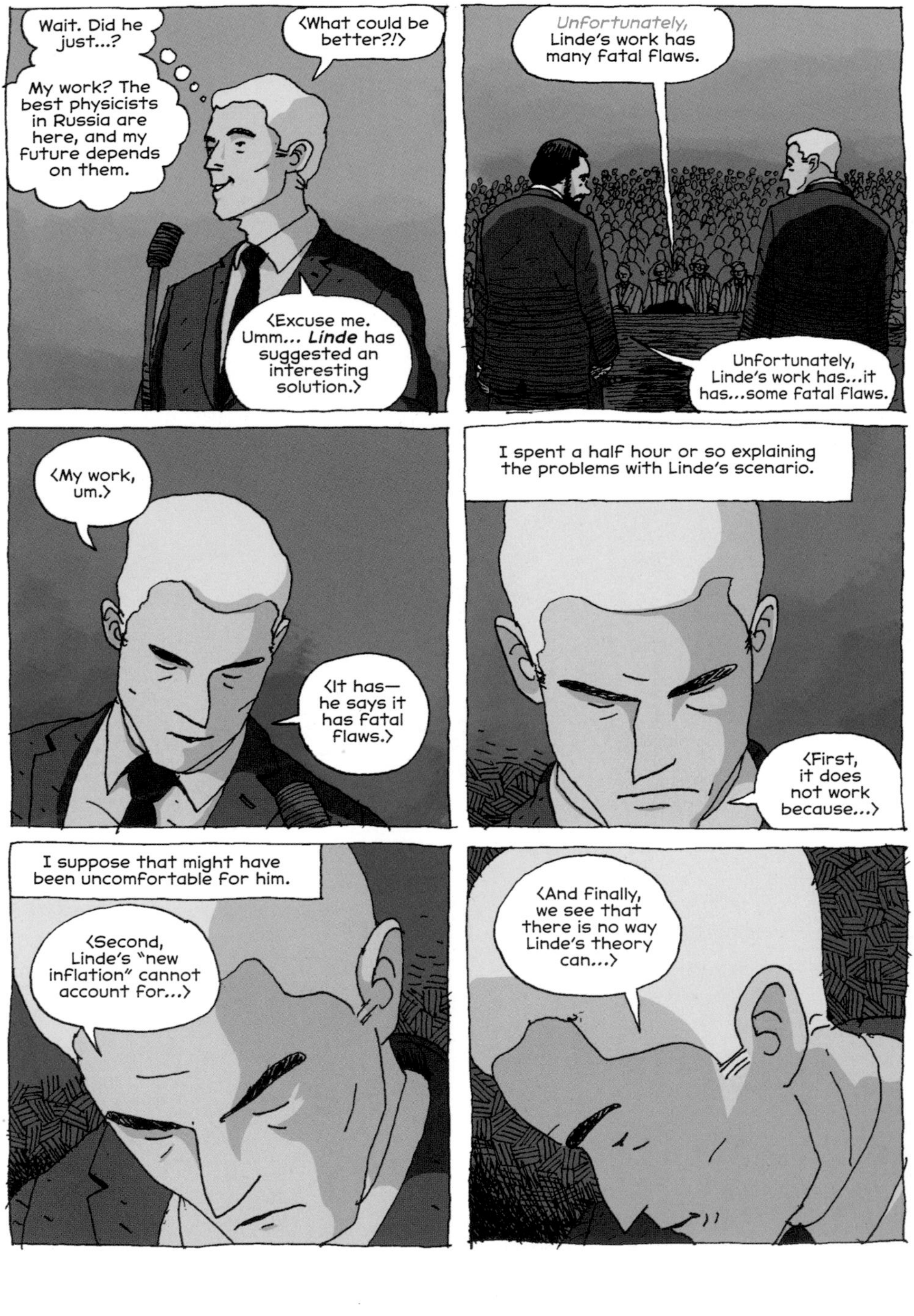
Wait. Did he just...?
My work? The best physicists in Russia are here, and my future depends on them.
<What could be better?!>
<Excuse me. Umm... *Linde* has suggested an interesting solution.>
Unfortunately, Linde's work has many fatal flaws.
Unfortunately, Linde's work has...it has...some fatal flaws.
<My work, um.>
<It has— he says it has fatal flaws.>
I spent a half hour or so explaining the problems with Linde's scenario.
<First, it does not work because...>
I suppose that might have been uncomfortable for him.
<Second, Linde's "new inflation" cannot account for...>
<And finally, we see that there is no way Linde's theory can...>

When I was done, Linde spoke in his own defense.

I'm not sure what he said, since he did so in Russian.

<I would like to respond, in brief. I have translated Professor Hawking, but I do not agree with him.>

Afterward, Linde approached me directly.

Can we discuss your problems with my theory further? In private?

It took a couple of hours. The official hosts were in a panic about the "famous British scientist who has disappeared."

You *did* not say *that* before.

Again, why *did* you not say *that* *before*?

<Academician Linde. What have you done with Dr. Hawking? If he has been harmed, the consequences for you will be worse than just embarrassment.>

<Harmed?>

<See for yourself. We're heading to Stephen's hotel now to continue the discussion.>

<He has invited me to Cambridge.>

...

<*Invited* doesn't mean *going*, Linde.>

CARR GUTH LINDE THORNE WHEELER SCIAMA STAROBINSKY PAGE ELLIS ZEL'DOVICH KAKU CARTER PENROSE HARTLE PERRY BEKENSTEIN REISSNER

I hosted a summer workshop on inflation a year later.

I was able to convince the Russian authorities to allow Andrei and other promising young scientists to come.

189

Starobinsky, now an elder statesman, spoke up often, though his stutter made the poor fellow difficult to understand.

‹cough cough›

Can you repeat that?

W-w-w-what I am t-t-t-trying to say is...

Many Americans came as well, including Alan Guth. We worked for two weeks straight.

That w-w-w-won't work because...

The *problem is with the* particle *physics.*

Eventually we all arrived at the same conclusion. Even with the new inflation models, the lumpiness of the universe we calculated was...

Too large.

The problem *is* with the *particle* physics.

I-I-I've been t-t-t-trying to t-t-tell you this all a-along.

In all our scenarios based on current theory, **everything** should end up as a black hole.

The problem *is with the* particle physics.

What? Oh. "The problem is with the particle physics..." Quantum theory.

Merging particle physics with our work on gravity didn't produce the "theory of everything" we all wanted.

CARR
THORNE
WINE
PERRY
BEER
PAGE
STAROBINSKY

As those two weeks had shown, it didn't even produce a working universe.

We parted company not knowing if we could bring together quantum theory and general relativity, but if we did?

We might have the answer to our big questions.

What kind of universe do we live in?

How *did it* begin?

Pardon?

‹cough cough cough›

And...is... *there...a...* God?

...

I thought we agreed to disagree. Or just not to discuss that.

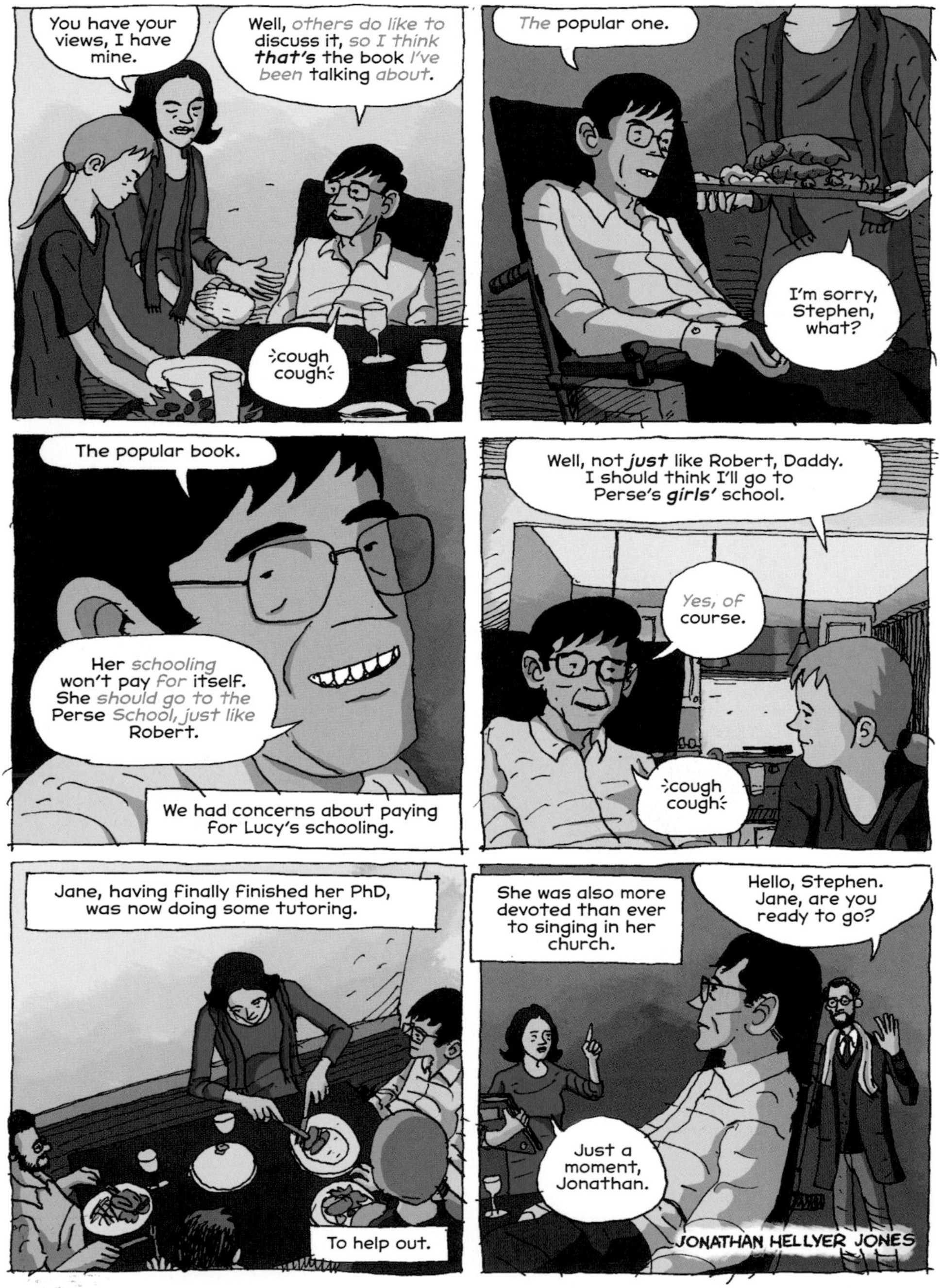
You have your views, I have mine.
Well, others do like to discuss it, so I think that's the book I've been talking about.
:cough cough:
The popular one.
I'm sorry, Stephen, what?
The popular book.
Her schooling won't pay for itself. She should go to the Perse School, just like Robert.
We had concerns about paying for Lucy's schooling.
Well, not just like Robert, Daddy. I should think I'll go to Perse's girls' school.
Yes, of course.
:cough cough:
Jane, having finally finished her PhD, was now doing some tutoring.
To help out.
She was also more devoted than ever to singing in her church.
Hello, Stephen. Jane, are you ready to go?
Just a moment, Jonathan.
JONATHAN HELLYER JONES

Everything all right?

Yes, of course.

We didn't talk about church.

When we did, it never went very well.

He's thinking about writing another book. A best seller, rather than a textbook.

Write a book? How would that...

Slowly. But if he says he'll do it, he'll do it.

I started with early ideas about the universe.

Most people **prefer** to *believe that the universe has* existed Forever *because this avoids* awkward *questions about the initial data on what* happened before *the beginning.*

I'm sorry, what comes before "prefer"?

Most people.

⸝cough cough cough⸝

"Most people." Right.

And then there was something about belief before "existed."

To believe that the universe has.

Okay, "believe that the universe... has"?

It took some time to develop the ideas.

But eventually we had a chapter or two for Cambridge University Press to consider.

SIMON MITTON, EDITOR

"...universe has existed forever because this avoids awkward questions about the initial data and about what happened before the beginning."

193

No commercial niche (1982–1985)

"This was the accepted picture when Einstein formulated general relativity..."

Etc., etc., "cosmological constant," etc., etc., and you close with "The mystery is why it should be so small."

Stephen, you see, *already* it's too specialized.

Highbrow. Readers don't *care* about cosmological constants.

But...

÷cough÷

There's no *commercial* niche for this.

It's like food. Baked beans. The blander the flavor, the broader the market.

I didn't want it to be bland, but I did want it to be commercial.

The kind of book sold in airports.

It took some time, but I revised the text.

From the start of civilization, man *has asked questions such as* "When *did the* universe begin?" "What happened *before the beginning?" "Will it have* an end?"

I'm sorry, before, um, "civilization," it was...?

"From the start of civilization, man has asked questions such as 'When did the universe begin?' 'What happened before the beginning?' 'Will it have an end?'"

"In most early cosmologies or mythologies, man was created by a deity or deities who had human forms and characters and who behaved in an arbitrary, and often malevolent manner."

Better.

* More than 1,000, actually. Many more...

1

When...*regular* people look at a book in a shop, they just flick through it before deciding if they want to read it.

They'll look at this and say, "This book has got *sums* in it," and put it right back.

We'd like to do this with you, really we would, but as it stands?

I think he's wrong. It's not "too technical."

And the equations are essential. They're where the truth and...and the *beauty* are.

After thinking about this, I concluded he was right.

Simon Mitton, that is.

Equations are just the boring part of mathematics anyway.

Equations *are just the* boring *part of mathematics* anyway.

So I revised again.

Chapter 1: Early Ideas About the Universe.

"Early Ideas About the Universe"?

⸕cough cough⸕

Around then the *New York Times* wrote an article about me, which led to some media attention.

Stephen, about the woman from MGM/UA?

There's another letter from her. We perhaps should respond in *some* way.

...

Say no.

Neither I nor my family would have any self-respect left if we let ourselves be portrayed by actors.

"I do not think that I would like to be the subject of a play, and I would not be interested in participating in the project in any way."

Fame is a nuisance. Even more letters began to come in, about all sorts of things.

Theories with nothing whatsoever to back them up.

Nothing but unfounded faith *in the theorist's* genius.

...

Yes, dear.

‹cough›

But the attention's not all bad.

‹cough cough cough›

By a *curious* coincidence, the attitude of City Council toward access for the disabled has taken a turn.

‹cough cough cough›

They answer *our* letters, at least. They might even get around to doing something.

Would that it had happened before years had passed of pushing the wheelchair with tiny children in tow.

And do you know an "Al Zuckerman"? From America?

Stephen, stop doing physics and listen.

An editor at Bantam Books had also read that *New York Times* article.

He recommended an agent—this Zuckerman—contact me.

If you haven't signed a contract already, he says Bantam Books is interested.

Have you? Signed, I mean?

Cambridge University press had just offered a £10,000 advance.

I know you might have wished for more, but we've never offered this much to anyone.

Not by a good margin, in fact.

Thank you.

So I...thought I'd come over with the good news myself, you see.

And a contract. Shall I leave it here, or with Judy?

Here *is* fine.

It was a good offer. But Bantam published Ray Bradbury, Ursula Le Guin, Star Trek novels. That sort of thing.

* Norton was flush from the success of *Surely You're Joking, Mr. Feynman!*

Books that sell in airports.

A bidding war between them and Norton resulted.*

‹cough cough›

Bantam won, with an offer considerably higher than Cambridge's.

$250,000.

It turned out to be a good bet for them.

I'm sorry, Simon. You just missed him.

No, probably not today.

Yes, I know, and I have given him your message.

Yes, of course— messages. Plural. So sorry.

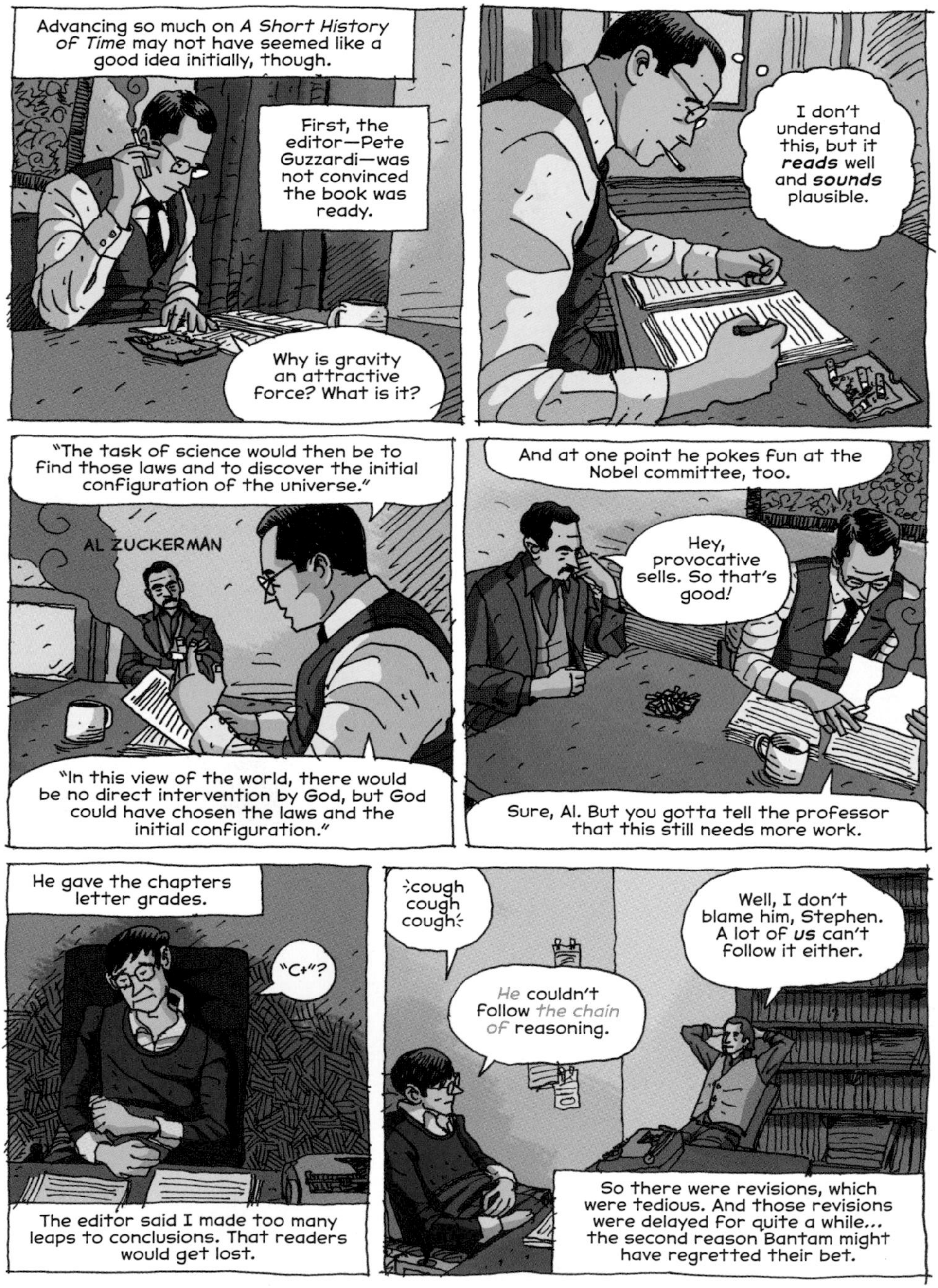

Advancing so much on *A Short History of Time* may not have seemed like a good idea initially, though.
First, the editor—Pete Guzzardi—was not convinced the book was ready.
Why is gravity an attractive force? What is it?
I don't understand this, but it ***reads*** well and ***sounds*** plausible.
"The task of science would then be to find those laws and to discover the initial configuration of the universe."
AL ZUCKERMAN
"In this view of the world, there would be no direct intervention by God, but God could have chosen the laws and the initial configuration."
And at one point he pokes fun at the Nobel committee, too.
Hey, provocative sells. So that's good!
Sure, Al. But you gotta tell the professor that this still needs more work.
He gave the chapters letter grades.
"C+"?
The editor said I made too many leaps to conclusions. That readers would get lost.
cough cough cough
He couldn't follow *the chain of* reasoning.
Well, I don't blame him, Stephen. A lot of ***us*** can't follow it either.
So there were revisions, which were tedious. And those revisions were delayed for quite a while... the second reason Bantam might have regretted their bet.

In 1985 my research took me to Switzerland to work with colleagues at CERN, regarding the particle accelerator.

RAYMONDE LAFLAMME

LAURA GENTRY

Jane no longer had to accompany me on every trip to help. I had friends and students fulfilling that role.

WHIRRRZZZZ

She, along with her friend Jonathan, took a bit of a holiday.

We planned to meet up for the *Ring* cycle at the Bayreuth Festival.

Typical. This says that Wagner set up this festival to showcase his own music.

Bad enough that it's Wagner in the first place. So... oppressive.

We still shared our love of music, after all.

Unfortunately, my health took a bad turn while in Geneva.

;cough cough cough cough COUGH;

Pneumonia.

I was taken to Hôpital Cantonal de Genève. But because they were camping, Jane didn't find out right away.

...calling to see what train he'll be on.

Induced *what?*

Yes. Immediately!

Oh my God.

Oh my God.

201

It will be all right, Jane. I'm sure of it. He's always recovered before.

Take the bags to the hotel, please.

URGENCES

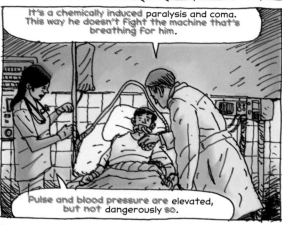

It's a chemically induced paralysis and coma. This way he doesn't fight the machine that's breathing for him.

Pulse and blood pressure are elevated, but not dangerously so.

It's good to talk to him.

He may not respond, but we think people in this state can hear us.

Perhaps we could speak outside?

They're saying we have to leave, Jane.

Out here in the hall will be fine.

We have some things we should discuss.

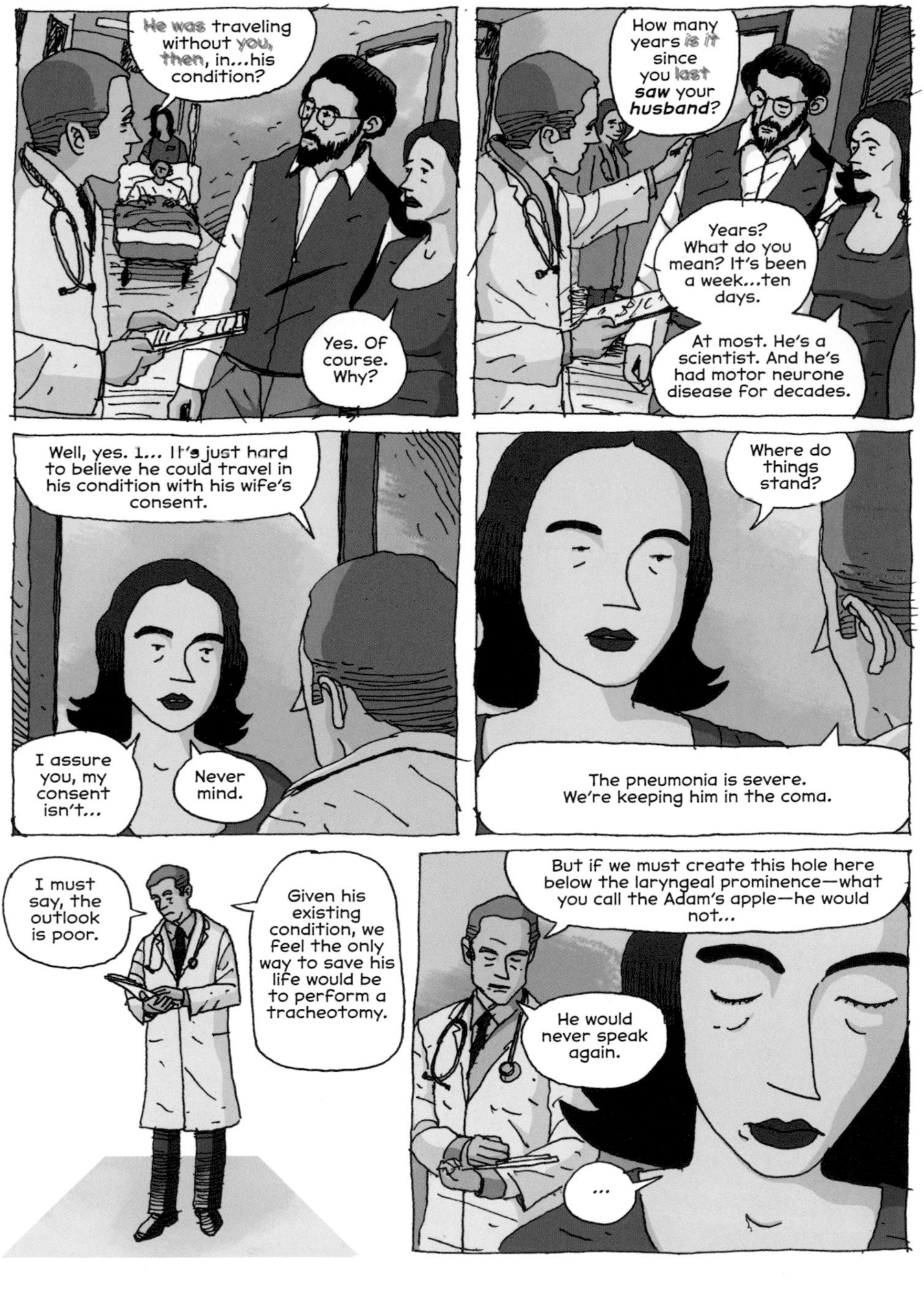
He was traveling without you, then, in...his condition?
Yes. Of course. Why?
How many years is it since you last *saw* your *husband*?
Years? What do you mean? It's been a week...ten days.
At most. He's a scientist. And he's had motor neurone disease for decades.
Well, yes. I... It's just hard to believe he could travel in his condition with his wife's consent.
I assure you, my consent isn't...
Never mind.
Where do things stand?
The pneumonia is severe. We're keeping him in the coma.
I must say, the outlook is poor.
Given his existing condition, we feel the only way to save his life would be to perform a tracheotomy.
But if we must create this hole here below the laryngeal prominence—what you call the Adam's apple—he would not...
He would never speak again.
...

Or, perhaps. Well...

Or *what*?

It is difficult to talk about, but in such situations we suggest that the family consider whether disconnecting life support is... appropriate.

It is your decision.

What sort of life?

I will leave you and your friend.

Jane.

Would you like to be alone?

Around-the-clock care from now on.

We can't afford that.

It will be so hard.

I'm tired.

Stephen must live.

Jane?

Stephen must live.

Stephen must live.

You must bring him around from the anesthetic.

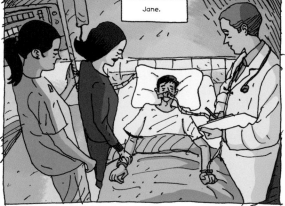

Jane.

September 1985

After I was able to breathe again on my own, I was taken by air ambulance back to Cambridge.

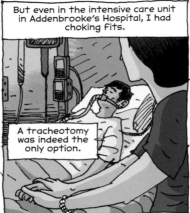

But even in the intensive care unit in Addenbrooke's Hospital, I had choking fits.

A tracheotomy was indeed the only option.

Count backward from ten, please.

10...9...8...7...6...5...4...

I had vivid dreams afterward.

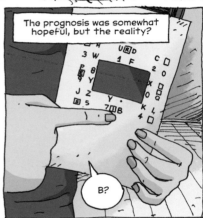

The prognosis was somewhat hopeful, but the reality?

B?

O.

O.

K.

"Book."

Which book?

It was tedious.

The 24-hour care I required was expensive. The National Health Service would pay for a nursing home, but...

...Kip convinced me to try to get *more* help, from the MacArthur Foundation. Murray Gell-Mann was on their board.

That worked, so I hired full-time nursing help.

ELAINE MASON

This one?

I was able to come home in November, and soon after that more good luck and help came from California.

A man named Walt Woltosz had created a speech synthesizer program—"Equalizer"—for his mother-in-law. He heard about my problem, and sent it to me.

This one?

I didn't want to use it at first.

But it was now clear that I wouldn't speak again, and I was too weak and ill to resume my research.

So I practiced. It has letters to spell out words, of course.

Please turn the page.

And menus of commonly used words and phrases. Common for me, anyway.

It also learns new combinations. For instance, "black" is often followed by "hole." Again, for me.

206

People spread a rumor that I also have a menu of insulting remarks.

CLICK

Please turn the page.

After a short while I was up to 15 words a minute—still a bit slow...

...but I think slowly, so it suited me quite well.

CLICK
CLICK
CLICK

My nurse Elaine's husband kitted out my wheelchair with a small computer and synthesizer.

It doesn't sound like a Dalek. Which is good.

The bad news is it gives me an American accident.*

HELLO.

* The voice is called Perfect Paul, which the company describes as "clear and logical"... Other possibilities were Huge Harry (loud), Doctor Dennis (quiet warmth), and Eeprom Ernie (??).

But it allowed me to continue my work.

Thank you for seeing me first, Professor. Here's where things stand with my—

BRIAN WHITT

CLICK CLICK
CLICKCLICKCLICK

HELLO. WILL YOU HELP ME FINISH MY BOOK?

That is what we did.

It was more urgent than ever.

Guzzardi kept asking questions...

He gives the "Curved Space" chapter a B+ and then asks "Can we envisage the big bang as 'the other side' of a black hole?"

ZZNT

I DO NOT KNOW WHAT THAT MEANS.

He also pushed for more illustrations, which was fine.

Most of the interesting ideas could be explained in words and pictures.

I worried about analogies, though.

THEY MUST BE SUFFICIENTLY ACCURATE THAT IF A PERSON THINKS IN THOSE TERMS, THEY DO NOT THEN EXTRAPOLATE THE ANALOGY AND MAKE NONSENSE OF IT.

Turtles all the way down to the mind of God (1986–1988)

Sunday night dinner often proved a good time to test some of them.

Hello, Mum. Brought some friends along for dinner.

Of course you did.

You're all welcome. The food's just arrived.

Hi Jonathan. Dad—

Hello, Mrs. Hawking.

Hello, Mrs. Hawking.

I enjoyed the company, even though they teased me about my diet.

Mmm. You can just taste the gluten, can't you? Not as good as Mum's, but...

VERY FUNNY.

And sometimes the discussions went in unexpected directions. For me.

You have to make assumptions, though, don't you? You have to decide what model of the universe to pursue, without knowing you're right.

So choosing a hypothesis to test involves a leap of faith, doesn't it?

...

ZZNT

I... ...SUPPOSE THERE IS SOME COMPARISON.

Is that a *concession* I hear? That even scientists rely on faith?

THERE IS SOME INTUITION INVOLVED. YES. FAITH IS PERHAPS AN APPROPRIATE METAPHOR.

BUT.

BUT WHAT FOLLOWS AFTER THAT LEAP IS DIFFERENT. THE MODEL IS TESTED AGAINST OBSERVATION.

AGAINST EXPERIMENT.

Experiments on black holes won't happen anytime soon, though. So you're left with...

An interesting metaphor.

As we finished the book, we had many similar discussions with Bantam as well.

I'D LIKE TO INCLUDE A MATHEMATICAL APPENDIX.

Your friend Mitton at Cambridge Press was right about equations, Stephen.

They would terrify people. And I hope you'll agree to my suggestion for the title.

I heard he had a new voice. It's...well, he doesn't sound like Darth Vader with a head cold anymore, at least.

I don't know. Vader might have been a good marketing angle.

Anyway, I think it's very close now. We're ready to send it to Dr. Sagan, if that's okay.

Carl Sagan was a big name in America, and Bantam asked him to write an introduction.

He was happy to do it. That and more, it turns out.

HE IS EDITING NOW TOO?

ZZNT

Well... Dr. Sagan's notes are just suggestions, I think.

211

He offers a different punch line for the story about Bertrand Russell and the turtles.

BROCA'S BRAIN

CARL SAGAN

It's the one he used in one of his own books, I think.

He corrected the spelling on a number of scientists' names.

And... so on. Most of this makes sense. I'll handle them.

Umm.

But in the conclusion, he... um, corrects the story about Laplace. You have him saying "These were left to God."

Sagan says Laplace told Napoleon that there was no *need* for God in his hypotheses.

And where you talk about quantum effects, he says "Quantum indeterminacy is to me more like the intervention of the Devil than of God."

"But if the latter, perhaps the reason is to limit our powers."

212

PERHAPS SAGAN IS RIGHT.

I WILL THINK ABOUT HIS SUGGESTIONS.

CLICK CLICK CLICK

THANK YOU.

ZZNT

Ultimately, I decided to end the book optimistically, about the quest for a complete theory of the universe.

TAKTAKTAK TAKTAK TAKTAK TAKTAK TAKTAK

...IF WE DO DISCOVER A COMPLETE THEORY, IT SHOULD IN TIME BE UNDERSTANDABLE IN BROAD PRINCIPLE BY EVERYONE, NOT JUST A FEW SCIENTISTS.

THEN WE SHALL ALL BE ABLE TO TAKE PART IN THE DISCUSSION OF WHY IT IS THAT WE AND THE UNIVERSE EXIST.

TAKTAKTAKTAK TAKTAK TAKTAK TAKTAK

"And if we find the answer to that, it would be the ultimate triumph of human reason."

"For then..."

213

"For then we would know the mind of God."

... It is certainly...

Well.

In the proof stage, I nearly cut that last sentence.

Had I done so, the sales for the book might have been halved.

Pete Guzzardi's change to the title helped sales too, I'm sure.

My original was *From the Big Bang to Black Holes: A Short History of Time.* He switched the order and changed *Short* to *Brief.*

I was not sure about that. But it made people smile, which I liked.

Others were not so confident. Guzzardi left Bantam shortly before the book came out, and the new editor got cold feet.

He reduced the initial print run to 40,000—all of which should have been pulped because of errors in the captions and images.

Oh dear.

Hello, Stephen? This is Don. Yes, very well, thank you. I wanted to let you know I got the book.

Yes. Yes. I...have to tell you I noticed a few things, though.

Oh, you already... Really!

But when Bantam tried to recall the book, they found that they had all sold.

Bantam had done marketing, of course, but not their usual. Simon Mitton had cautioned me that they might push the wrong angle for the book.

"Aren't cripples marvelous?" and all that.

NEW YORK

WHIRRRZZZZZ

But even though I don't much like the picture they chose for the cover, the marketing was tasteful—no skywriting or T-shirts.

And things have gone rather well ever since.

WHIRRRZZZZZ

Our privacy was compromised somewhat by all of this, of course.

"Fair Lucy, will you marry me? But read my thesis to your father first!"

Other letters contained more serious offers. About six months after the book came out, a fellow named Gordon Freedman wrote me.

He's a film producer. I thought you already said no to that.

I DO NOT WANT TO DO A FILM ABOUT MY LIFE.

BUT IF IT IS ABOUT THE SCIENCE OF MY BOOK, I MAY CONSIDER IT.

What about the proposal to do another book? An autobiography?

We could collaborate on it, perhaps.

CLICK CLICK
CLICK CLICK CLICK

I SHOULD BE GLAD OF YOUR OPINION.

ZZNT

I traveled to Israel while the book was still climbing the sales charts— Roger and I were to receive a prize there.

It was my first experience with real fame.

THE WAILING WALL

Professor Hawking, what does your research tell you about the existence of God?

Is there room for God in the universe you describe?

Do you believe in God?

NO.

217

If I may. The way I see it, there are many ways to find God...

The questions about science were similar to the ones about God. Always the same...

Could one of you explain for our readers what a black hole is?

Stephen?

A BLACK HOLE IS IN ONE SENSE THE SIMPLEST TYPE OF OBJECT IN THE UNIVERSE. IT ONLY HAS CHARGE, SPIN, AND MASS.

QUITE A LOT OF MASS, THOUGH.

Sometimes my students and friends get frustrated with these questions, since most could be answered by *any* physicist, or with just a little research on the part of the questioner.

But I do not usually mind.

People are curious about the big questions...

The density of the Dead Sea is roughly 1.2 kilograms per liter.

Quite dense, though a far cry from infinity per liter like a black hole, Professor.

Heh.

But it's far greater than the human body nonetheless.

...and they realize that science can provide answers.

Well, most bodies! What do you feed him, by the way? He weighs a *ton* for such a slight chap.

It's all in his brain.

Though scientists don't always agree on what those answers *are*.

Some of my fellow scientists considered that a problem with my book—they complained that I confused the laity by mixing established theory with my own opinion.

And that I, through the cover photograph, had exploited my disability.

And...that there were problems of giving proper credit. One was regarding my account of Andrei Linde and his inflationary theory.

Wait a minute.

DAVID RITTENHOUSE LABORATORY

This time it was not Linde that was embarrassed. Instead it was Paul Steinhardt, a professor in Pennsylvania.

Upon returning from Russia I had given a lecture where I mentioned Linde's work, and some people interpreted a passage in my book as saying that I thought Steinhardt had gotten his idea from me.

PAUL STEINHARDT

Wait. "I was therefore rather surprised when... he sent me a paper... in which they proposed something very similar to Linde's idea." Is he serious?

What?

Many friends who were there assured me I hadn't mentioned Linde's work at all.

I was sure I had, but it couldn't be proven either way, so I apologized.

"I have never doubted your assertion that you had not been aware of Linde's idea."

"I included the story just as an illustration of the way science is done."

I do not want to do a film about my life. (1989–1990)

"I am very sorry if some people have got the wrong impression from what I wrote."

Hmm. I suppose it will have to do.

It took quite a while to sort out, but in the end I published a note in *Physics Today* about it, and we changed the next printing of the book.

That next printing happened soon. It sold quite well, even though scientists and book critics alike—baffled by its popularity—kept saying that most people didn't actually *read* it.

ROWN BOOKS

And if they did, they couldn't have understood it.

These critics feel they are very clever people. And if they can't understand *A Brief History of Time?* Well, then ordinary mortals have no chance.

I think some of that is rather patronizing.

In part, that's why the film project went forward, with Steven Spielberg involved.

ERROL MORRIS

STEVEN SPIELBERG

ELSTREE STUDIOS, HERTFORDSHIRE

I agreed because a film might reach more people, people who would watch it all the way through, and because I was convinced that director Errol Morris would not lose sight of the science.

Not everyone was interested in participating.

Elaine declined to be interviewed on camera, as did Jane...

Jane felt she had answered enough questions since the book came out, perhaps.

He is...

He is delving into realms that really do matter to thinking people...and in a way that can have a very disturbing effect.

And he's not competent.

No, no. Not in that way, of course. The physical aspect is one we've all accepted.

Do you take milk with your tea?

I suppose so, yes. Having 24-hour nursing may have felt like giving in to his condition. An admission of defeat.

But for me it means I'm no longer solely responsible for his care.

I suppose my role now is simply to tell him he's not God.

CLICK

For myself, the film was a lot better than I thought it might be.

ZZNT

But when I saw the first cut of it, I was horrified by how my voice sounded.

WHICH CAME FIRST, THE CHICKEN OR THE EGG?

And I told Errol Morris that the beginning was ridiculous.

I was also concerned about the mention of *imaginary time*, which was not explained in the film.

RAYMOND LAFLAMME

IT IS PRESENTED AS A BIT OF SCIENTIFIC MUMBO JUMBO OR MAGIC.

I had nearly decided not to mention imaginary time in the book, and was conscious that I did not explain it very well there, either.

I thought if we couldn't do better in the film, maybe we should leave it out.

ROLEX
OYSTER
COSMOGRAPH

After all, if the idea is to get people to watch science, it is important that the science be good...

...OTHERWISE THE WHOLE EXERCISE IS NOT WORTH THE EFFORT.

I also didn't think we needed to assume that people have an attention span of only two minutes, after which the science had to be interrupted by some anecdote.

223

I think people can take more than that, provided their interest is aroused. Not that I object to anecdotes...

CLICK CLICK

I WAS BORN EXACTLY 300 YEARS AFTER THE DEATH OF GALILEO.

I ESTIMATE THAT ABOUT 200,000 OTHER BABIES WERE ALSO BORN THAT DAY.

CLICK

CLICK

I DON'T KNOW WHETHER ANY OF THEM WAS LATER INTERESTED IN ASTRONOMY.

Unfortunately, the movie's debut in England aired opposite both a snooker championship and *Jeeves and Wooster*.

The producer called the ratings "dismal."

But the 1.7 million people who did watch? They watched it all the way through. He told me that is unusual.

They expected better ratings in the US.

While on a visit in 1990 we decided my bet on Cygnus X-1.

Actually, Kip wasn't as certain as I was, but I'd seen enough evidence to conclude that there **was** a black hole there.

So while he was away in Moscow, I snuck in and conceded.

Meanwhile the book remained a best seller, and attention remained high.

Some of it was quite gratifying.

I was made a Companion of Honour of the British Empire in 1989.

"In action faithful and in honor clear."

THANK YOU, MA'AM.

We... Stephen... would like to present you with a copy of his book. He has signed it, in his own manner.

I'm not sure how familiar the queen actually was with my work, though.

Is it a popular account of his work such that a lawyer might give?

Lawyer?

LAWYER?

No, ma'am. It is more readable than that. Especially the first chapters...

The conversation quickly turned to my computer's American accent. It was perhaps a bit awkward.

Jane and I separated not long after that... just before our 25th anniversary.

We kept this quiet so as to avoid unwanted attention.

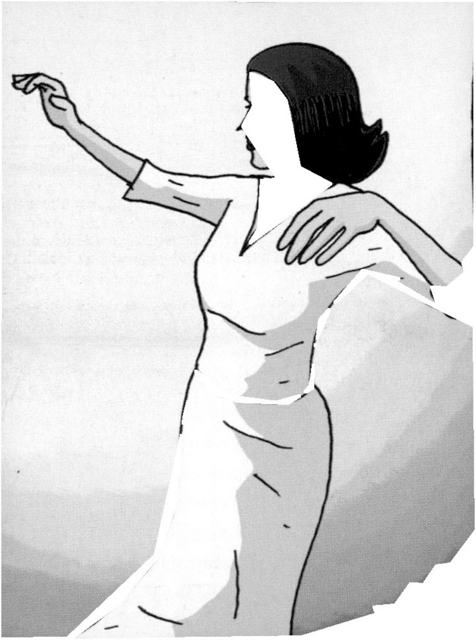

Jonathan Hellyer Jones and Jane had grown rather close.

Elaine and I had as well. We'd moved in together soon after the separation and married in 1995.

That was the same year *A Brief History of Time* came out in paperback. Some questioned the need for that.

By now the hardcover has sold one copy for every 750 men, women, and children in the world. What's more—

SO THERE ARE 749 TO GO.

Professor Stephen Space Time Publica University of Camb Cambridge CB3 9EW ited Kingdom.

ZZNT

In the meantime, I had also published *Black Holes and Baby Universes*, a book of essays.

And that wasn't all…

WHAT IS THIS CHECK?

It's from your agent, for the next book. Why was it sent here rather than home?

THE BOOK OF ESSAYS?

What? No, the other book.

WHAT OTHER BOOK?

It was a movie tie-in, an idea I had heard about but thought had been dropped.

TELL HIM I OBJECT VERY MUCH TO HIS SENDING ME MONEY FOR A BOOK THAT IS TO GO OUT UNDER MY NAME BUT THAT I HAVE NOT SEEN.

IT WAS QUITE WRONG TO GO THIS FAR WITHOUT CONSULTING ME.

I DON'T LIKE THE IDEA OF PUTTING MY NAME ON SOMETHING I HAVE NOT WRITTEN.

LEGS.

But in the end, I reconciled with the *Reader's Companion*...

IT IS THE BOOK OF THE FILM, OF THE BOOK.

BANTAM BOOKS

I DON'T KNOW HOW MANY ITERATIONS OF THIS THEY ARE PLANNING, BUT I'M AFRAID THE NEXT THING WILL BE A FILM OF THE BOOK OF THE FILM OF THE BOOK.

WE... ...ESSOR ST... ...KING

It was a busy time.

I began speaking in front of many more student groups.

Even though the questions I get are similar, I try not to just save old answers and give the same one every time.

Has your disability helped you do your work?

ZZNT

WELL, I DO NOT HAVE TO TEACH CLASSES LIKE OTHER PROFESSORS.

AND I AM SURE MY DISABILITY IS PART OF THE REASON I HAVE BECOME WELL-KNOWN.

I FIT THE IMAGE OF A DISABLED GENIUS, BUT THAT IS MEDIA HYPE.

I AM NOT A GENIUS LIKE EINSTEIN.

I of course also tried to keep up with my field...

NO, NO, NO, NO.

SUE MASSEY, PERSONAL ASSISTANT

CLICK CLICK CLICK CLICK

YES, OKAY.

CLICK CLICK

NO, NO, NO, NO.

...and to continue my own research program as well.

In 1992, in response to some work done by Kip, I had proposed the "chronology protection conjecture."

"Chronology Protection Conjecture"
Phys. Rev. D, vol. 46: 603–611. (1992)

CAN YOU HEAR ME?

THERE HAVE BEEN A NUMBER OF SUGGESTIONS THAT WE MIGHT BE ABLE TO WARP SPACE-TIME IN SUCH A WAY AS TO ALLOW RAPID INTERGALACTIC SPACE TRAVEL, OR TO TRAVEL BACK IN TIME.

$$ds^2 = -dt^2 + 2f\,dt\,d\phi -$$
$$+ r^2(d\theta^2 + \sin^2\theta\,d\phi$$
$$f = r^2t^2\sin^4\theta\,\sin^2\left[\frac{\pi r}{L}\right].$$

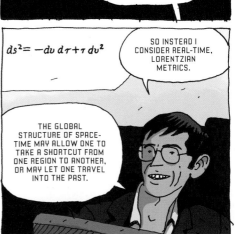

ONE MIGHT THINK THAT SUCH TRAVEL COULD BE POSSIBLE USING THE WORMHOLES THAT APPEAR IN THE EUCLIDEAN APPROACH TO QUANTUM GRAVITY.

HOWEVER, ONE WOULD HAVE TO BE ABLE TO MOVE IN THE IMAGINARY DIRECTION OF TIME TO USE THESE WORMHOLES... NO GOOD FOR SPACE OR TIME TRAVEL.

$$ds^2 = -dv\,d\tau + \tau\,dv^2$$

SO INSTEAD I CONSIDER REAL-TIME, LORENTZIAN METRICS.

THE GLOBAL STRUCTURE OF SPACE-TIME MAY ALLOW ONE TO TAKE A SHORTCUT FROM ONE REGION TO ANOTHER, OR MAY LET ONE TRAVEL INTO THE PAST.

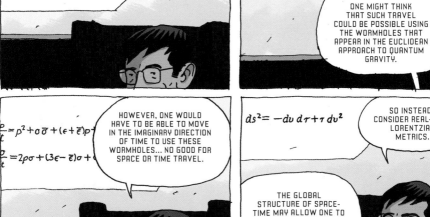

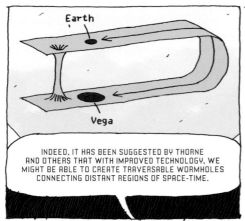

Earth

Vega

INDEED, IT HAS BEEN SUGGESTED BY THORNE AND OTHERS THAT WITH IMPROVED TECHNOLOGY, WE MIGHT BE ABLE TO CREATE TRAVERSABLE WORMHOLES CONNECTING DISTANT REGIONS OF SPACE-TIME.

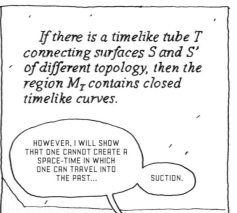

If there is a timelike tube T connecting surfaces S and S' of different topology, then the region M_T contains closed timelike curves.

HOWEVER, I WILL SHOW THAT ONE CANNOT CREATE A SPACE-TIME IN WHICH ONE CAN TRAVEL INTO THE PAST...

SUCTION.

I concluded this way:

IT SEEMS THERE IS A "CHRONOLOGY PROTECTION AGENCY," WHICH PREVENTS THE APPEARANCE OF CLOSED TIMELIKE CURVES AND MAKES THE UNIVERSE SAFE FOR HISTORIANS.

THERE IS ALSO STRONG EXPERIMENTAL EVIDENCE IN FAVOR OF MY CONJECTURE FROM THE FACT THAT WE HAVE NOT BEEN INVADED BY HORDES OF TOURISTS FROM THE FUTURE.

RRRRZZZZZZ

The question-and-answer sessions after my talks went on for a while. I had to remind audiences about the time it took for me to compose responses. I suggested they chat among themselves, or read newspapers...relax.

Stephen. Could you clarify what happens with the null geodesic?

WHIRRRRZZZZZZ

CLICK CLICK CLICK CLICK

AS ONE APPROACHES A CLOSED NULL-GEODESIC GAMMA IN THE CAUCHY HORIZON, THE PROPAGATOR WILL ACQUIRE EXTRA SINGULARITIES FROM NULL GEODESICS CLOSE TO GAMMA THAT ALMOST RETURN TO THE ORIGINAL POINT.

Okay, right. Thanks.

Ha ha.

Ha ha.

Would you be willing to bet on this?

Ha ha.

WHIRRRRZZZZZZ

234

CLICK CLICK CLICK

WHIRRRRZZZZZZ

WHIRRRRZZZZZZ

YES.

Higgs (1996–2008)

Kip would not take this wager, though.

I enjoy betting with you, but only when I have a reasonable chance of winning.

And my strong gut feeling is that I would lose this one.

I *was* able to make some other wagers, though. I bet Gordy Kane $100 that CERN wouldn't find the Higgs boson with its Large Electron-Positron Collider.

In fact, I had expressed doubt that the Higgs could ever be found...

ORGANISATION EUROPÉENNE POUR LA RECHERCHE NUCLÉAIR (CERN), GENEVA

I didn't think a failure to do so was a bad thing, necessarily.

I THINK IT WILL BE MUCH MORE EXCITING IF WE DON'T FIND THE HIGGS. THAT WILL SHOW SOMETHING IS WRONG, AND THAT WE NEED TO THINK AGAIN.

SUCTION.

WELCOME TO

When I won that bet, I bet Gordy a further $100 that CERN's new Large Hadron Collider also wouldn't find it. I should have quit while I was ahead...

NFERENCE

All of this didn't sit so well with Peter Higgs.

Hawking?

It is difficult to *engage him* in discussion, so he has got away with pronouncements in a way that other people would not.

236

Also, his celebrity status gives him instant credibility that others do not have.

It wasn't *just* pronouncements, though. I wrote a paper titled "Virtual Black Holes" that predicted there would be no Higgs boson.

Peter thought my physics was bad.

I have read a paper he wrote, which I think is the basis for the kind of calculation he does.

And frankly, I don't think the way he does it is good enough.

"God particle" or no "God particle," I wanted the LHC to succeed, since even if it didn't find the Higgs boson, it might generate microscopic black holes...

...and they would generate Hawking radiation.

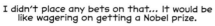

I didn't place any bets on that... It would be like wagering on getting a Nobel prize.

JOHN PRESKILL

Besides, it is unlikely that one could ever definitively settle such a bet.

Which is not unlike most things in cosmology, I suppose.

$$c^2 dr^2 = -\left(\frac{dr^2}{\Delta} + d\theta^2\right) \rho^2 + \left(c\, dt - a\sin^2\theta\, d\phi\right)^2 \frac{\Delta}{\rho^2} - \left((r^2 + a^2)\, d\phi - ac\, dt\right)^2 \frac{\sin^2\theta}{\rho^2}$$

Finkelstein Time

SINGULARITY

Even so, Kip and John Preskill did bet me that naked singularities exist.

The loser will...okay, I've got it... the loser will reward the winner with clothing to cover the winner's nakedness.

Yes. That's good.

And the clothing is to be embroidered with a suitable concessionary message.

Roger didn't join me in that wager, even though he and I agreed about singularities.

Some of our other ideas about space and time had diverged since the golden age of cosmology, however.

We'd held a public debate about them.

Hawking & Penrose: The Nature of Space &Ti

ISAAC NEWTON INSTITUTE FOR MATHEMATICAL SCIENCES, CAMBRIDGE

"The Nature of Space and Time" (1994)

CAN YOU HEAR ME?

ROGER AND I DIFFER IN OUR APPROACH TO QUANTUM GRAVITY AND, INDEED, TO QUANTUM THEORY ITSELF.

I AM REGARDED AS A DANGEROUS RADICAL BY PARTICLE PHYSICISTS, BUT...I AM DEFINITELY A CONSERVATIVE COMPARED TO ROGER.

I TAKE THE POSITIVIST VIEW THAT A PHYSICAL THEORY IS JUST A MATHEMATICAL MODEL AND THAT IT IS MEANINGLESS TO ASK WHETHER THAT THEORY CORRESPONDS TO REALITY.

ZZNT

ALL THAT ONE CAN ASK IS THAT ITS PREDICTIONS ARE IN AGREEMENT WITH OBSERVATION.

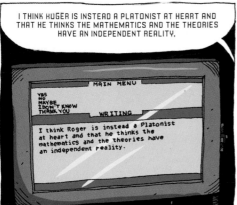

I THINK HUGER IS INSTEAD A PLATONIST AT HEART AND THAT HE THINKS THE MATHEMATICS AND THE THEORIES HAVE AN INDEPENDENT REALITY.

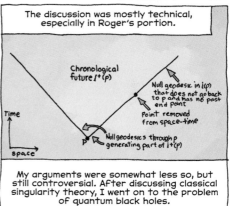

The discussion was mostly technical, especially in Roger's portion.

My arguments were somewhat less so, but still controversial. After discussing classical singularity theory, I went on to the problem of quantum black holes.

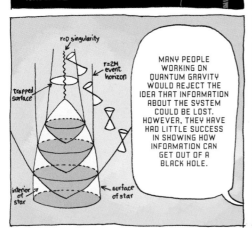

MANY PEOPLE WORKING ON QUANTUM GRAVITY WOULD REJECT THE IDEA THAT INFORMATION ABOUT THE SYSTEM COULD BE LOST. HOWEVER, THEY HAVE HAD LITTLE SUCCESS IN SHOWING HOW INFORMATION CAN GET OUT OF A BLACK HOLE.

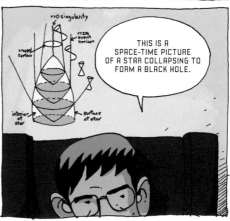

THIS IS A SPACE-TIME PICTURE OF A STAR COLLAPSING TO FORM A BLACK HOLE.

GOVERNMENT CUTS HAVE MEANT THAT CAMBRIDGE UNIVERSITY CAN ONLY AFFORD TWO-DIMENSIONAL SCREENS.

I HAVE THEREFORE SHOWN TIME IN THE VERTICAL DIRECTION AND USED PERSPECTIVE TO SHOW TWO OF THE THREE SPACE DIRECTIONS.

CLICK CLICK

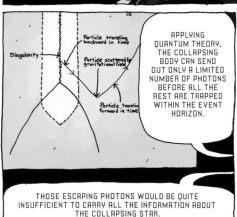

APPLYING QUANTUM THEORY, THE COLLAPSING BODY CAN SEND OUT ONLY A LIMITED NUMBER OF PHOTONS BEFORE ALL THE REST ARE TRAPPED WITHIN THE EVENT HORIZON.

THOSE ESCAPING PHOTONS WOULD BE QUITE INSUFFICIENT TO CARRY ALL THE INFORMATION ABOUT THE COLLAPSING STAR.

THUS, THERE'S NO WAY AN OUTSIDE OBSERVER CAN MEASURE THE STATE OF THAT COLLAPSED BODY.

WHIRRRRZZZZZ

ONE MIGHT NOT THINK THIS MATTERS MUCH, BECAUSE THE INFORMATION WOULD STILL BE INSIDE.

BUT AS I WILL SHOW, BLACK HOLES RADIATE AND LOSE MASS AND EVENTUALLY DISAPPEAR COMPLETELY, TAKING THE INFORMATION WITH THEM.

THIS INFORMATION REALLY IS LOST AND DOESN'T COME BACK.

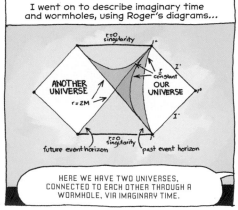

I went on to describe imaginary time and wormholes, using Roger's diagrams...

HERE WE HAVE TWO UNIVERSES, CONNECTED TO EACH OTHER THROUGH A WORMHOLE, VIA IMAGINARY TIME.

240

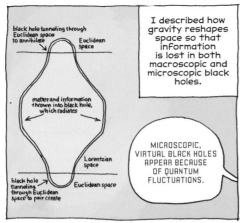

I described how gravity reshapes space so that information is lost in both macroscopic and microscopic black holes.

MICROSCOPIC, VIRTUAL BLACK HOLES APPEAR BECAUSE OF QUANTUM FLUCTUATIONS.

PARTICLES AND INFORMATION CAN FALL INTO THESE HOLES AND GET LOST.

SO GRAVITY INTRODUCES A NEW LEVEL OF UNPREDICTABILITY, OVER AND ABOVE THE UNCERTAINTY OF QUANTUM THEORY.

MAYBE THAT'S WHERE ALL THE MISSING SOCKS WENT.

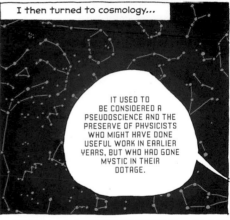

I then turned to cosmology...

IT USED TO BE CONSIDERED A PSEUDOSCIENCE AND THE PRESERVE OF PHYSICISTS WHO MIGHT HAVE DONE USEFUL WORK IN EARLIER YEARS, BUT WHO HAD GONE MYSTIC IN THEIR DOTAGE.

Initially, there were no observations to support their work, but technology has changed all that.

CLICK CLICK CLICK CLICK CLICK

WHIRRRRZZZZZZ

A more serious objection is that cosmologists have to make assumptions about the initial conditions of the universe—and those initial conditions are questions for metaphysics or religion, not science.

ZZNT

THE THEOREMS ROGER AND I PROVED HAVE MADE THE SITUATION WORSE.

WE SHOWED THAT CLASSICAL RELATIVITY BRINGS ABOUT ITS OWN DOWNFALL— IT PREDICTS THAT IT CAN'T PREDICT THE UNIVERSE.

HOWEVER, MY NO-BOUNDARY PROPOSAL, DEVELOPED WITH JIM HARTLE, SOLVED THIS.

ONE CAN PARAPHRASE THE PROPOSAL AS "THE BOUNDARY CONDITION OF THE UNIVERSE IS THAT IT HAS NO BOUNDARY."

The proposal implies things about the differences between the beginning and end of time—the expansion-contraction cycle of the universe.

TO ILLUSTRATE, RAYMOND, WILL YOU PLEASE DRAW A FOUR-DIMENSIONAL SPHERE FOR US?

The universe would start smooth and ordered and would get more disordered and irregular as it expanded.

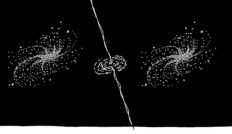

However, I thought it would have to return to a smooth and ordered state as it got smaller.

This would have implied that the thermodynamic arrow of time would have to reverse in the contracting phase.

CUPS WOULD MEND THEMSELVES AND JUMP BACK ON THE TABLE. PEOPLE WOULD GET YOUNGER, NOT OLDER, AS THE UNIVERSE GOT SMALLER AGAIN...

IT IS NOT MUCH GOOD WAITING FOR THE UNIVERSE TO COLLAPSE AGAIN TO RETURN TO OUR YOUTH. THAT WILL TAKE TOO LONG...

...BUT IF THE ARROW OF TIME REVERSES WHEN THE UNIVERSE CONTRACTS, IT MIGHT ALSO REVERSE INSIDE BLACK HOLES.

I WROTE A PAPER CLAIMING THE ARROW OF TIME WOULD REVERSE WHEN THE UNIVERSE CONTRACTED AGAIN.

BUT DISCUSSIONS WITH DON PAGE AND RAYMOND LAFLAMME CONVINCED ME THAT THE UNIVERSE WOULD NOT RETURN TO A SMOOTH STATE IN THE COLLAPSE.

HOWEVER, I WOULDN'T RECOMMEND JUMPING INTO A BLACK HOLE AS A WAY OF PROLONGING ONE'S LIFE.

I HAD MADE MY GREATEST MISTAKE.

AT LEAST IN PHYSICS.

CLICK CLICK

ZZNT

I concluded my lectures with what I consider the two most remarkable features I have learned in my research.

(1) GRAVITY CURLS UP SPACE-TIME SO THAT SPACE-TIME HAS A BEGINNING AND AN END.

$d = 1/2 \, gt$

(2) THERE IS A DEEP CONNECTION BETWEEN GRAVITY AND THERMODYNAMICS BECAUSE GRAVITY ITSELF DETERMINES THE TOPOLOGY OF THE SPACE ON WHICH IT ACTS.

QUANTUM GENERAL RELATIVITY, TOGETHER WITH THE NO-BOUNDARY PROPOSAL, PREDICTS A UNIVERSE LIKE THE ONE WE OBSERVE.

COSMIC CENSORSHIP MAY SHIELD US FROM BLACK HOLE SINGULARITIES, BUT WE SEE THE BIG BANG IN FULL-FRONTAL NAKEDNESS.

WHIRRRRZZZZZZ

HOWEVER, EVEN THOUGH QUANTUM THEORY RESTORES THE PREDICTABILITY THAT CLASSICAL THEORY LOST, IT DOES NOT DO SO COMPLETELY.

WE CANNOT SEE THE WHOLE OF SPACE-TIME ON ACCOUNT OF BLACK HOLE AND COSMOLOGICAL EVENT HORIZONS, AND INFORMATION IS LOST BEHIND THOSE EVENT HORIZONS.

THIS INTRODUCES AN EXTRA LEVEL OF UNPREDICTABILITY, BUT IT MAY ALSO BE WHY THE UNIVERSE APPEARS TO US THE WAY IT DOES.

SO, TO HAVE REMOVED PREDICTABILITY FROM PHYSICS AND THEN TO HAVE PUT IT BACK AGAIN, EVEN IN A REDUCED SENSE, IS QUITE A SUCCESS STORY.

I REST MY CASE.

CLICK CLICK CLICK CLICK

ZZNT

An unsuitable concession (1997)

$$\begin{pmatrix} z^0 \\ z^1 \end{pmatrix} = \frac{i}{\sqrt{2}} \begin{pmatrix} r^0 + r^3 & r^1 + ir^2 \\ r^1 - ir^2 & r^0 - r^3 \end{pmatrix} \begin{pmatrix} z^2 \\ z^3 \end{pmatrix}$$

Roger spoke as well, of course, and gave his view of space-time.

As always, Stephen poses some excellent, if awkward, points. To answer I shall introduce some two-spinor notation to explain the basis of twistor correspondence.

This is where people usually get confused.

Some characterized our discussion as a continuation of the debates Einstein and Bohr had—casting me as Niels Bohr.

That made Roger "Einstein," perhaps based on his idea that theories and their underlying mathematics are objectively real.

Others might have reversed our roles—but either way is flattering, of course.

The debate resulted in a book—one that did not require nearly so much work as *A Brief History* had...

...or any of the other hypothetical books people were proposing I write.

A sequel? They must be kidding.

AGREED. WHAT WOULD I CALL IT? *A LONGER HISTORY OF TIME? SON OF TIME?*

Not everyone agreed with me regarding *information loss* from black holes, though. So on a visit to Caltech, I made another bet with Kip and John Preskill. This time Kip and I were on the same side.

Um...Kip, Stephen.

Kip and I firmly believed that information swallowed by a black hole is hidden forever from the outside universe.

Black hole

Event horizon

Singularity

Observer

Observer's line of sight

No. Information can never be revealed even as the black hole evaporates and completely disappears.

Okay, fine. I'd say "Whereas I firmly believe that a mechanism for the information to be released by the evaporating black hole *must* and *will* be found."

Found in the *correct* theory of quantum gravity.

WHIRRZ

The terms were more technical, involving an initial pure quantum state collapsing to form a black hole, and then that black hole evaporating into a pure quantum state.

Observer

Observer's line of si—

$$R\,p,q+1$$

$$ds^2 = \sum_{i=1}^{p} dx_i^2 - \sum_{j=1}^{q+1} dt_j^2$$

$$\sum_{i=1}^{p} x_i^2 - \sum_{j=1}^{q+1} t_j^2 = -\alpha^2$$

The stakes were easy to understand, though.

Black hole

Observer

E— ho

S:

The loser(s) will reward the winner(s) with an encyclopedia of the winner's choice.

CLICK CLICK CLICK

CLICKCLICKCLICK

CLICK CLICK

FROM WHICH INFORMATION CAN BE RECOVERED AT WILL.

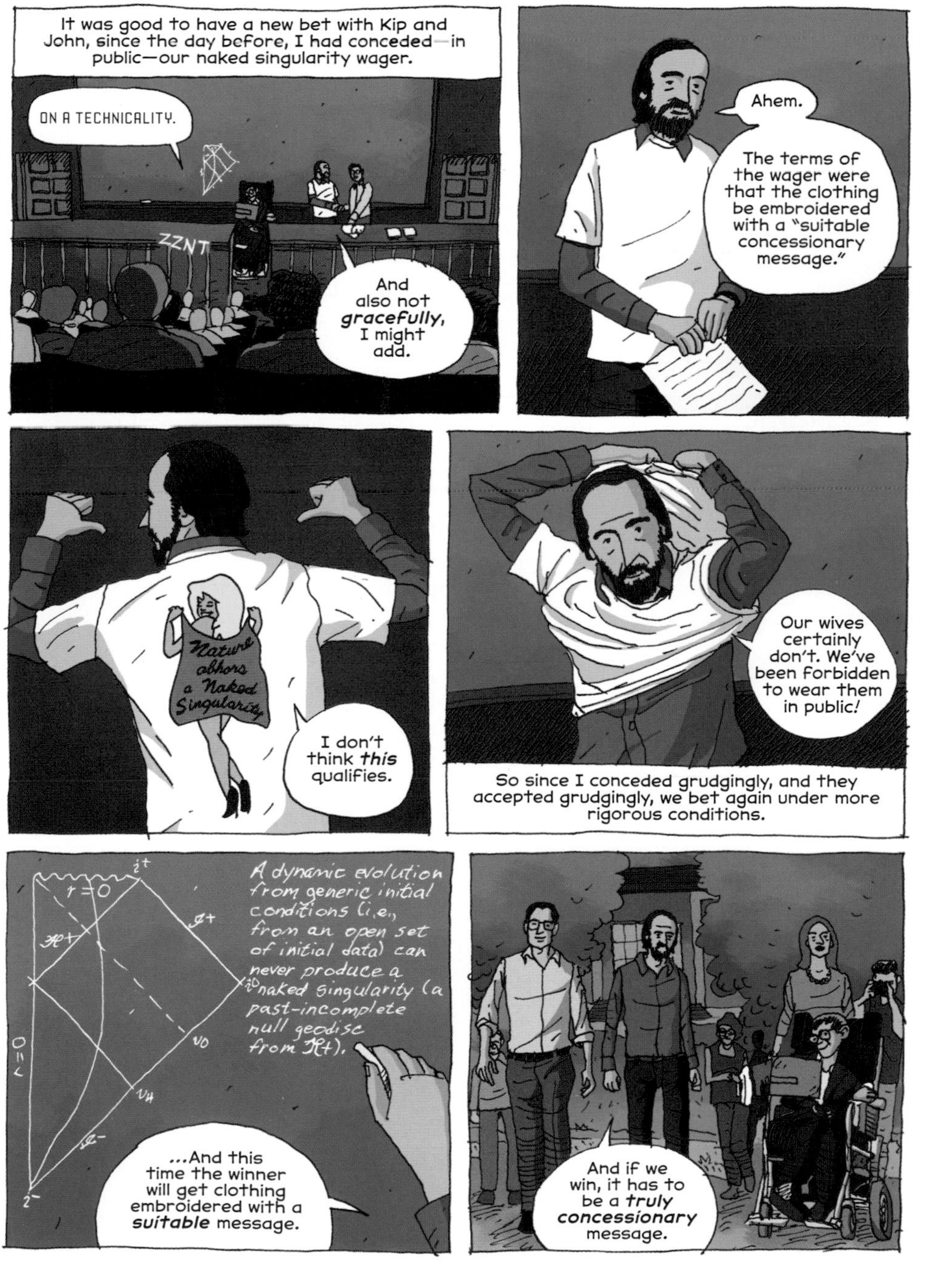

It was good to have a new bet with Kip and John, since the day before, I had conceded—in public—our naked singularity wager.
ON A TECHNICALITY.
ZZNT
And also not *gracefully*, I might add.
Ahem.
The terms of the wager were that the clothing be embroidered with a "suitable concessionary message."
Nature abhors a Naked Singularity
I don't think **this** qualifies.
Our wives certainly don't. We've been forbidden to wear them in public!
So since I conceded grudgingly, and they accepted grudgingly, we bet again under more rigorous conditions.
A dynamic evolution from generic initial conditions (i.e., from an open set of initial data) can never produce a naked singularity (a past-incomplete null geodisc from ℐ+).
...And this time the winner will get clothing embroidered with a *suitable* message.
And if we win, it has to be a *truly concessionary* message.

The edge of the world (1997)

Kip and I went to Antarctica that year.

ESCENARIO →

WHIRRZZZ

On the way, I stopped in Chile and gave a lecture.

They opened with very loud rock music. It was right after civilian rule was established, so the stage behind me was filled with both the new civilian government and military brass.

There was tension in the air...

Si. Si. Si. CAN YOU HEAR ME? Si. Si. Si.

...but the talk was well received.

Then we flew to King George Island in Antarctica.

I wanted to visit the end of the world.

Stephen, wait.

It was filled with TV cameras, journalists, and physicists.

My wheelchair didn't work well there, even with snow chains.

But they had snowmobiles.

WHIRRRZZZZZZ

It was one of the most exciting things I've done.

WHIRRRRZZZZZZ

And trips like this help me make my point about my no-boundary proposal.

When people ask, "How can the universe be finite but still unbounded?"

I can tell them this...

IN ALL MY TRAVELS, I HAVE NOT MANAGED TO FALL OFF THE EDGE OF THE WORLD.

ZZNT

The Universe in a Nutshell (2001)

I didn't actually get to the South Pole, though...

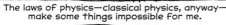

The laws of physics—classical physics, anyway— make some things impossible for me.

Or at least, impractical. For example, the house I built with Elaine.

It has two stories. She insisted on that, but I of course can't get to the second floor on my own.

ELAINE. HOW HAVE YOU—

Not *now*, Stephen.

—BEEN.

WHIRRRRZZZZZZ

It is beautiful, though.

My book *The Universe in a Nutshell* came out in 2001.

I wrote it in between doing my own research, public appearances, and some appearances on television.

For instance, I helped advertise the Quantum Jazzy 1400 wheelchair.

IT WILL KEEP MY NURSES FIT AS THEY TRY TO KEEP UP.

WHIRRRRZZZZZ

The book didn't sell as well as *A Brief History of Time*, but the probability of that was small to begin with.

It had eight times as many equations, for one thing.

STEPHEN HAWKING

THE UNIVERSE IN A NUTSHELL

This did not mean it sold only 40,000 copies, though.

It did quite a bit better than that, so each equation doesn't necessarily reduce my sales by one half.

Like an updated version I'd done of *A Brief History of Time*, this was more heavily illustrated and in color.

It also addressed new developments in physics, some quite speculative...

...some of which Kip and I had discussed at his 60th birthday symposium in 2000.

I'd talked about time travel and the Feynman sum-over-histories technique. And as a gift, I presented him with a calculation.

$$10^{60}$$

THE PROBABILITY THAT KIP CAN GO BACK IN TIME USING A WORMHOLE IS ONE IN TEN...

...ONE IN TEN WITH A TRILLION TRILLION TRILLION TRILLION TRILLION ZEROS AFTER IT.

THAT'S A PRETTY SMALL PROBABILITY, BUT IF YOU LOOK AT KIP, YOU MAY SEE A SLIGHT FUZZINESS AROUND THE EDGES.

THIS CORRESPONDS TO THE FAINT POSSIBILITY THAT SOME BASTARD FROM THE FUTURE CAME BACK AND KILLED HIS GRANDFATHER, SO KIP'S NOT REALLY THERE.

In return, he made some predictions about the discovery of gravitational waves and direct observation of black holes.

Sometime between 2002 and 2008, Earth-based gravitational wave detectors will watch black holes collide.

253

They will also watch their collisions trigger wild vibrations of space-time warpage.

I should have bet him on that.

He also took some shots at my chronology protection conjecture and my calculations about wormholes.

They're based on a tentative, queasily infirm version of the laws of quantum gravity.

Though to be fair, *all* versions of the quantum gravity laws are queasily infirm today.

By 2020— if my predictions are right—they will be fully firm.

BUT THEY STILL WON'T ALLOW FOR BACKWARD TIME TRAVEL.

Normally Kip and I would be glad to bet on even 1 : 10⁶⁰ odds, but in this case we're on the same side.

And with regard to the new laws of quantum gravity?

I might take that bet. But perhaps I shouldn't.

I have already had to revise my predictions about such a thing— a Theory of Everything—once.

In my 1980 inaugural lecture as Lucasian Professor of Mathematics, I had said that the end of physics might be in sight.

A Theory of Everything? (1980, 2002)

The goal of *theoretical* physics might be achieved in the not-too-distant future.

By the end of the century we *might have a* complete, consistent, and *unified* theory of *all* physical interactions.

One *that would* describe all possible observations.

The lecture touched on many more things than that, of course, and much of it was forgotten in the excitement of the day.

I even forgot to sign the registry, adding my name to Newton's and Dirac's before me.

YES, I HAD SUGGESTED WE MIGHT FIND A COMPLETE UNIFIED THEORY BY THE END OF THE CENTURY.

OKAY, I WAS WRONG.

Pardon?

I WAS A BIT OPTIMISTIC TO HOPE THAT WE WOULD HAVE SOLVED THE PROBLEM BY THE END OF THE CENTURY.

CLICK CLICK

I STILL THINK THERE'S A 50-50 CHANCE THAT WE WILL FIND A UNIFIED THEORY IN 20 YEARS.

BUT THE 20 YEARS STARTS NOW.

I NO LONGER THINK THAT WILL BE THE END OF THEORETICAL PHYSICS, THOUGH. I NO LONGER EVEN THINK WE WILL HAVE A COMPLETE THEORY.

In my 2002 lecture "Gödel and the End of Universe" I noted that some people will be very disappointed if there is not an ultimate theory—a "theory of everything."

I used to belong to that camp.

I HAVE CHANGED MY MIND.

ARMS.

I'M NOW GLAD THAT OUR SEARCH FOR UNDERSTANDING WILL NEVER COME TO AN END, AND THAT WE WILL ALWAYS HAVE THE CHALLENGE OF NEW DISCOVERY.

WITHOUT IT, WE WOULD STAGNATE.

"Sixty Years in a Nutshell" (2002)

I almost didn't get to deliver any lectures that year, including at my 60th birthday celebration a few months earlier.

What happened?!

I BROKE MY HIP JUST AFTER CHRISTMAS.

... Hello, Elaine.

Are you doing okay, Stephen?

ADDENBROOKE'S HOSPITAL DID A VERY GOOD JOB OF PUTTING ME BACK TOGETHER AGAIN.

I began my "Sixty Years in a Nutshell" talk in a way intended to head off unwanted speculation.

CAN YOU HEAR ME?

AS YOU CAN SEE, IT WAS ALMOST 59.97 YEARS IN A NUTSHELL.

I HAD AN ARGUMENT WITH A WALL A FEW DAYS AFTER CHRISTMAS...

WHIRRRRZZZZZZ

...AND THE WALL WON.

HA HA.

Ha ha.

Ha ha.

Ha ha.

Ha ha.

Ha ha.

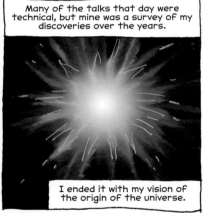

Many of the talks that day were technical, but mine was a survey of my discoveries over the years.

I ended it with my vision of the origin of the universe.

QUANTUM FLUCTUATIONS LED TO THE SPONTANEOUS CREATION OF TINY UNIVERSES OUT OF NOTHING.

MOST OF THEM COLLAPSE BACK TO NOTHING, BUT A FEW THAT REACH A CRITICAL SIZE WILL EXPAND IN AN INFLATIONARY MANNER.

THEY WILL FORM GALAXIES AND STARS, AND MAYBE BEINGS LIKE US.

...A GLORIOUS TIME TO BE ALIVE AND DOING RESEARCH IN THEORETICAL PHYSICS.

OUR PICTURE OF THE UNIVERSE HAS CHANGED A GREAT DEAL IN THE LAST 40 YEARS...

AND I'M HAPPY IF I HAVE MADE A SMALL CONTRIBUTION.

I want to share my excitement and enthusiasm.

In addition to the scientific birthday celebration, thanks to my wife and Richard Branson, later that year I got a balloon ride as a gift.

And I was also able to continue doing more lectures and appearances...

How do you make a legal signature if you can't write?

How do you feel about the Americans with Disabilities Act?

Will you write an autobiography?

I WOULD RATHER NOT GO INTO DETAILS OF MY PRIVATE LIFE.

What are Klingons really like?

CLICK CLICK

WELL, I HAVE ONLY MET ONE, AND THAT WAS TEN YEARS AGO, AFTER MY POKER SESSION WITH DATA, EINSTEIN, AND NEWTON.

Ha ha.

A RED ALERT BROKE UP THE GAME BEFORE I COULD COLLECT MY WINNINGS.

Even though I was unwilling to write an autobiography, I did write more books.

And I edited a few, and then I co-wrote one.

It had more pictures, and they were in color.

STEPHEN HAWKING with Leonard Mlodinow

A BRIEFER HISTORY OF TIME

The type was also larger and the line spacing a little farther apart than in the original.

260

"Information Loss in Black Holes"
Phys. Rev. D, vol. 72: 084013. (2005)

So it was less dense.

The book came out the same year as a more scientific paper I wrote, one concerning my bet with John Preskill.

I had conceded that bet the year before, at the GR17* conference in Dublin.

WHIRRRRZZZZZZ

* 17th International Conference on General Relativity and Gravitation

Yes, this is a last-minute addition. He sent a note saying "I have solved the black hole information paradox, and I want to talk about it."

CURT CUTLER, GR17'S ORGANIZER

I haven't seen his paper. To be quite honest, I said yes based on his reputation alone.

$\Psi[h_{ij}, \phi, \tau],$

$Z(\beta) = \int Dg D\phi e^{-I[g,\phi]} = Tr(e^{-\beta H}).$

$Z(E_0) = \int_{-i\infty}^{+i\infty} d\beta Z(\beta) e^{\beta E_0}.$

I talked about calculations others had done that pointed the way to a resolution of the information paradox. But their solutions didn't satisfy me, so I did my own.

The conclusion was the same, though.

singularities

THERE IS NO BABY UNIVERSE BRANCHING OFF INSIDE A BLACK HOLE, AS I ONCE THOUGHT. THE INFORMATION GOING INTO THE BLACK HOLE REMAINS FIRMLY IN OUR UNIVERSE.

261

I AM SORRY TO DISAPPOINT BOTH KIP AND SCIENCE FICTION FANS, BUT BECAUSE INFORMATION IS PRESERVED, THERE IS NO POSSIBILITY OF USING BLACK HOLES TO TRAVEL TO OTHER UNIVERSES.

IF YOU JUMP INTO A BLACK HOLE, YOUR MASS ENERGY WILL BE RETURNED TO OUR UNIVERSE...

...IN A MANGLED FORM THAT CONTAINS THE INFORMATION ABOUT WHAT YOU WERE LIKE...

...BUT IN AN UNRECOGNIZABLE STATE.

SO EVEN THOUGH IT IS NOT RETURNED IN A USEFUL WAY, INFORMATION IS NOT LOST.

LEGS.

I conceded my bet to Preskill, and presented him with a baseball encyclopedia.

I had offered one on cricket, but John is all-American. So I had *Total Baseball* flown in.

Well, I'm glad of course, even though it will be hard to get home. Maybe I should have asked for a CD-ROM instead of print.

But print is the right choice—it's heavy, like a black hole. And it takes much longer to get the information out—that's like a black hole too.

Yes, of course I accept. But I look forward to his paper, as I'm not sure I agree with Stephen's reasons for conceding.

Neither do I.

Kip did **not** concede the bet. If he agrees to do so later, he could pay me back...

When my paper came out, I concluded with a description of the state of information leaving a black hole.

IT IS LIKE BURNING AN ENCYCLOPEDIA. INFORMATION IS NOT LOST, BUT IT IS VERY HARD TO READ.

CHRISTOPHE GALFARD

I GAVE JOHN PRESKILL A BASEBALL ENCYCLOPEDIA. MAYBE I SHOULD HAVE GIVEN HIM THE ASHES.

SUCTION.

Perhaps that was less than truly concessionary.

Still, thinking that information is destroyed in black holes—*that* was my biggest blunder.

OR AT LEAST MY BIGGEST BLUNDER IN SCIENCE.

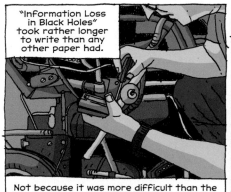

"Information Loss in Black Holes" took rather longer to write than any other paper had.

Not because it was more difficult than the others, really, or because I had to admit I was wrong. It was my because of my hands.

They had become too weak to use the clicker.

So I began using the Words+ "Infrared/ Sound/Touch" switch to speak.

Mounted on my glasses, I can activate it by moving my cheek muscle...

...or blinking my eye.

Is that comfortable, Stephen?

It was slower.

YES, THAT'S FINE. THANK YOU.

"I am often mistaken for Stephen Hawking." (2005–2006)

But it worked, and I was back to leading a normal life.

I returned to Israel the next year. I didn't get back to the Dead Sea, but I *was* able to make giving a lecture in Palestine a condition of my visit.

My first trip to that part of the world had been just before *A Brief History of Time* came out. Now I could not travel anonymously.

IT IS NOT ENOUGH FOR ME TO WEAR DARK GLASSES AND A BEARD.

THE WHEELCHAIR GIVES ME AWAY.

It is recognized everywhere I go.

Now that I was speaking via an infrared switch, they were added to things like the doors of my home so I could operate those on my own.

Just as well, as Elaine and I were divorced that year.

"Just a distraction" (2006)

To my surprise, the media took interest in this. To my annoyance, they sought out my children for comment.

It's not really my business to discuss— I'm not the one getting divorced.

My assistant Judith handled the press for me.

JUDITH CROASDELL

No statement.

He is *far* too busy. This is just a distraction that is really annoying. We don't have *any* time for *any* of this.

And we have *no* interest in *any* of the gossip.

I was very busy.

For instance, Lucy and I planned a trip to Beijing and Hong Kong together. I was attending a conference on string theory.

It was so difficult to control the crowds that we almost couldn't make it to our hotel.

The reception was wonderful.

I LIKE CHINESE CULTURE, CHINESE FOOD...

ZZNT

AND ABOVE ALL, CHINESE WOMEN. THEY ARE BEAUTIFUL.

我喜欢中国文化、中国食物，但最热爱的是中国女性。她们非常美。

The pollution was awful, and in answer to questions about it, I discussed the threat of global warming.

EARTH MIGHT END UP LIKE VENUS, AT 250 DEGREES CENTIGRADE AND RAINING SULFURIC ACID.

Some of the questions were personal as well.

你认为自己是个什么样的人？

She asks "How would you describe yourself?"

OPTIMISTIC, ROMANTIC, AND STUBBORN.

Returning home, we found our trip had generated some attention.

Oh dear. Again?

Is it always like this?

YES. I AM OFTEN MISTAKEN FOR STEPHEN HAWKING.

We used it to make an announcement.

How did you like Beijing?

How was the trip?

Would you comment on your divorce?

I LIKED CHINA VERY MUCH, THOUGH WE FOUND THE AIR QUALITY QUITE BAD.

AND WE'VE DECIDED TO DO A BOOK TOGETHER.

A book? Will this be Son of a Briefer History of Time?

And who is "we"?

NOT A SEQUEL TO ANYTHING. THIS WILL BE FOR YOUNGER READERS.

SUCTION.

I AM NOT WORKING WITH A SCIENTIST. I AM WORKING WITH MY DAUGHTER.

It came to me at my son William's seventh birthday party...

Stephen!

Stephen, Stephen.

Stephen, what would happen to me if I fell into a black hole? What would it feel like?

CLICK CLICKCLICKCLIK CLICK CLICK CLICK

ZZZNT

WELL, DO YOU LIKE SPAGHETTI?

Lucy got the idea from my answers to William's friend and got to work on a draft right away.

She's a good writer.

At one point I laughed so much, I fell out of my chair.

That's when I knew he was hooked...that he'd started to enjoy this.

270

For *George's Secret Key to the Universe*, my role was consulting scientist, ensuring it was accurate and educational.

I recruited short essays from Brandon Carter, Lord Martin Rees, Kip, and a few other friends for the next books. I also wrote one myself in the voice of "Eric," the main scientist character.

In the third book—*George and the Big Bang*—a mysterious group wants to destroy the Large Hadron Collider to stop the secrets of the early universe becoming known.

GEORGE AND THE BIG BANG

LUCY & STEPHEN HAWKING

...Yes, they propose quite a bit more than just color for the cover.

I came up with that plot myself.

Dad must have thought "What the hell, *I'm* writing the story."

Yes, right! Sorry...

Lucy! The boys! Little pitchers have big ears.

IT'S TRUE.

I WANT TO SHARE MY EXCITEMENT AND ENTHUSIASM.

ZZNT

THERE'S NOTHING LIKE THE EUREKA MOMENT OF DISCOVERING SOMETHING THAT NO ONE KNEW BEFORE.

I WON'T COMPARE IT TO—

Yes, Stephen, we *know*. Again, I must remind you...

Little pitchers.

My storyline for *George and the Big Bang* is unlikely. No scientist would destroy the LHC to stop discoveries being made. But my position hadn't changed since 1996...

IT WILL BE MUCH MORE EXCITING IF WE DON'T FIND THE SO-CALLED GOD PARTICLE.

I'm sorry, more exciting if we **don't** find it?

YES. THAT WILL SHOW THAT SOMETHING IS WRONG AND WE NEED TO THINK AGAIN.

SO I HAVE A BET OF $100 WITH GORDY KANE THAT WE WON'T DISCOVER THE HIGGS BOSON.

SUCTION.

For myself, I hoped that miniature black holes might be created, or Hawking radiation observed.

There was some media hype about those tiny black holes, and how if CERN produced them they might swallow the Earth.

I—along with Roger and Martin and some other colleagues—released a statement to assure people there was no danger.

THE WORLD WILL NOT COME TO AN END WHEN THE LHC TURNS ON.

Collisions releasing greater energy occur millions of times a day in the Earth's atmosphere, and nothing terrible happens.

IT IS ABSOLUTELY SAFE.

IF YOU ARE READING THIS, THEN MY COLLEAGUES AND I WERE RIGHT.

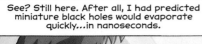
See? Still here. After all, I had predicted miniature black holes would evaporate quickly...in nanoseconds.

And with a burst of light from the Hawking radiation.

So a very small bang, in the grand scheme of things.

As for the bigger bang, the beginning of our universe is still my focus.

If the no-boundary proposal is correct, there would be no singularities and the laws of physics would hold everywhere, including at the very beginning of time and space.

IT IS A UNIVERSE THAT JUST IS.

THERE ARE OTHER THEORIES, INCLUDING EVOLUTIONARY ONES, WITH MULTIPLE UNIVERSES.

BUT I WANT TO FIND A SINGLE EXPLANATION...

...FOR A SINGLE UNIVERSE.

THAT'S WHY, AFTER I KNEW I HAD MOTOR NEURONE DISEASE, I CHOSE COSMOLOGY.

ALSO BECAUSE THE FIELD WAS UNDERDEVELOPED AT THE TIME, WITH LITTLE COMPETITION.

SO MY DISEASE WOULD NOT BE A SERIOUS IMPEDIMENT.

HÉLÈNE MIALET

Wait. I'm sorry, but previously... *here* you've said that you chose cosmology before knowing about the disease.

Which is correct?

THERE WERE LOTS OF EXCITING DISCOVERIES TO BE MADE, AND NOT MANY PEOPLE TO MAKE THEM.

NOW THERE IS MUCH MORE COMPETITION.

LEGS.

I'm sorry, but *which* is correct?

BY NOW, MOST PEOPLE ACCEPT THAT THE LAWS OF SCIENCE HOLD EVERYWHERE.

EXCEPT AT THE BEGINNING OF THE UNIVERSE.

BUT UNLESS ONE ALSO KNOWS WHAT LAWS HELD THEN, ONE DOESN'T KNOW WHAT UNIVERSE EMERGED FROM THE BIG BANG.

274

Controlling it (2006–2007)

I STILL HAVE AN URGE TO KNOW HOW THINGS WORK AND TO CONTROL THEM.

THAT IS WHY I'M MOST PROUD OF MY NO-BOUNDARY PROPOSAL, FORMULATED WITH JIM HARTLE.

IT EXPLAINS THE WHOLE HISTORY OF THE UNIVERSE. EVEN AT THE BIG BANG.

AND IF YOU UNDERSTAND HOW THE UNIVERSE OPERATES, YOU CONTROL IT.

IN A WAY.

ZZNT

Wait... what?

SO I DO NOT AGREE WITH THE VIEW THAT THE UNIVERSE IS A MYSTERY.

Okay. On a different note, what's the most common misconception about your work?

PEOPLE THINK I'M A *SIMPSONS* CHARACTER.

BEING A CELEBRITY CAN BE GRATIFYING, BUT IT DOESN'T LAST.

AND MY INTERESTS AND REPUTATION ARE IN SCIENCE.

THE ROYAL SOCIETY RECENTLY GAVE ME ITS OLDEST AWARD, THE COPLEY MEDAL, FOR OUTSTANDING CONTRIBUTIONS TO THEORETICAL PHYSICS AND THEORETICAL COSMOLOGY.

THAT IS GRATIFYING, AND MY FRIEND—AND PRESIDENT OF THE ROYAL SOCIETY— MARTIN REES PRESENTED IT TO ME.

As a special gift, NASA has flown it in space aboard space shuttle mission STS-121.

RICHARD BRANSON HAS PROMISED ME A FLIGHT ON HIS SPACESHIP AS WELL.

AND FOR THAT I MUST GET IN SOME TRAINING. PLEASE EXCUSE ME.

LOOK OUT. THERE IS AN ERROR IN YOUR CALCULATION OF TAU...

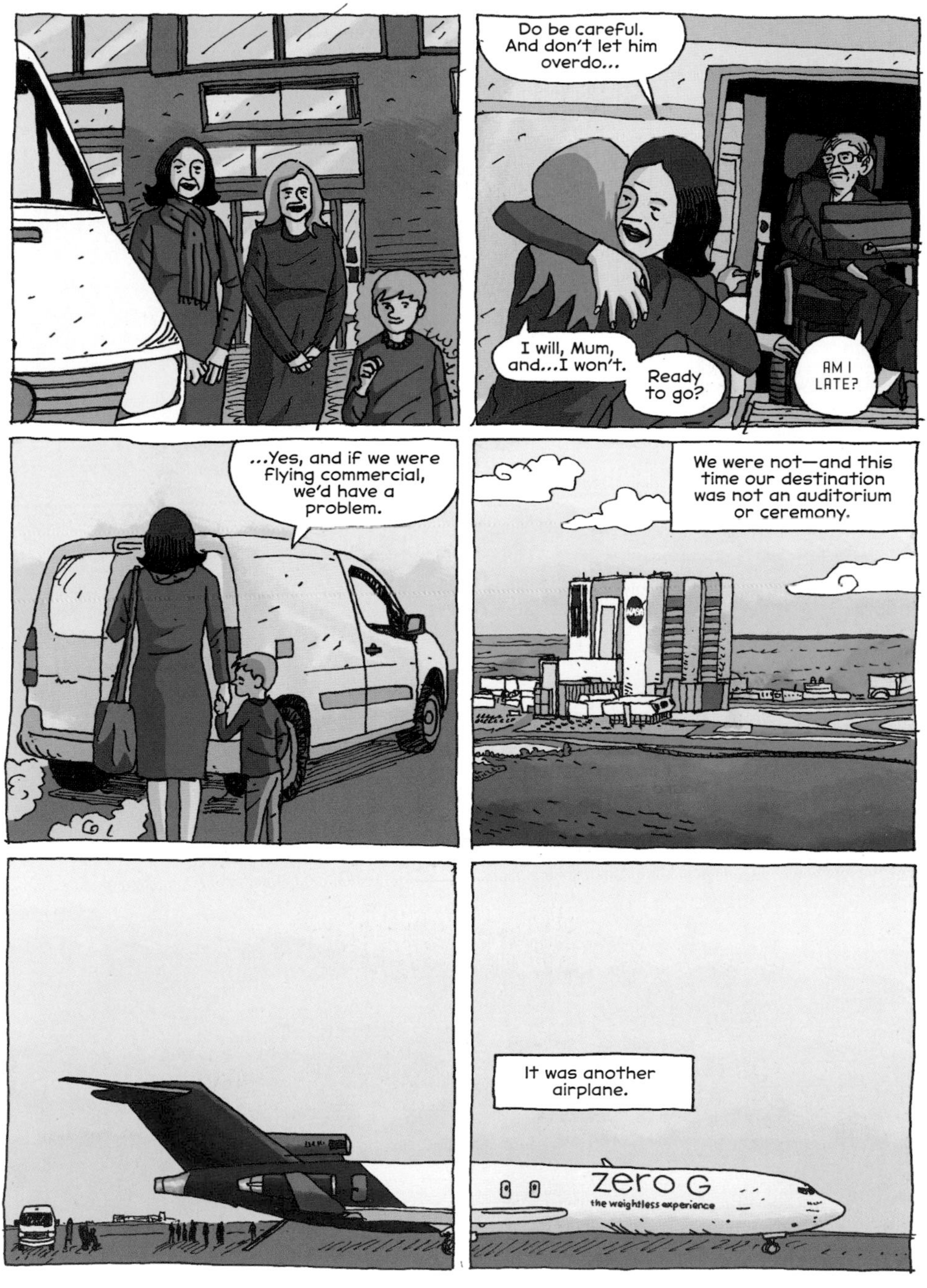

Do be careful. And don't let him overdo...
I will, Mum, and...I won't.
Ready to go?
AM I LATE?
...Yes, and if we were flying commercial, we'd have a problem.
We were not—and this time our destination was not an auditorium or ceremony.
It was another airplane.
zero G
the weightless experience

There will be a period of 2 g as we climb. You understand that, yes?

...

BLINK

V_{rel} is only 0.000001 c, so no relativistic effects...

I'm... quite sure...he understands what's involved.

Celebrity may not last, but it has benefits.

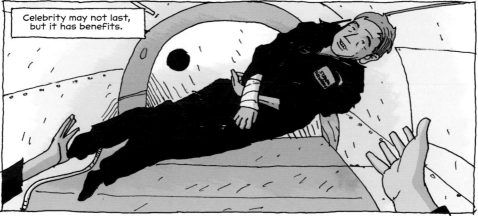

Again?

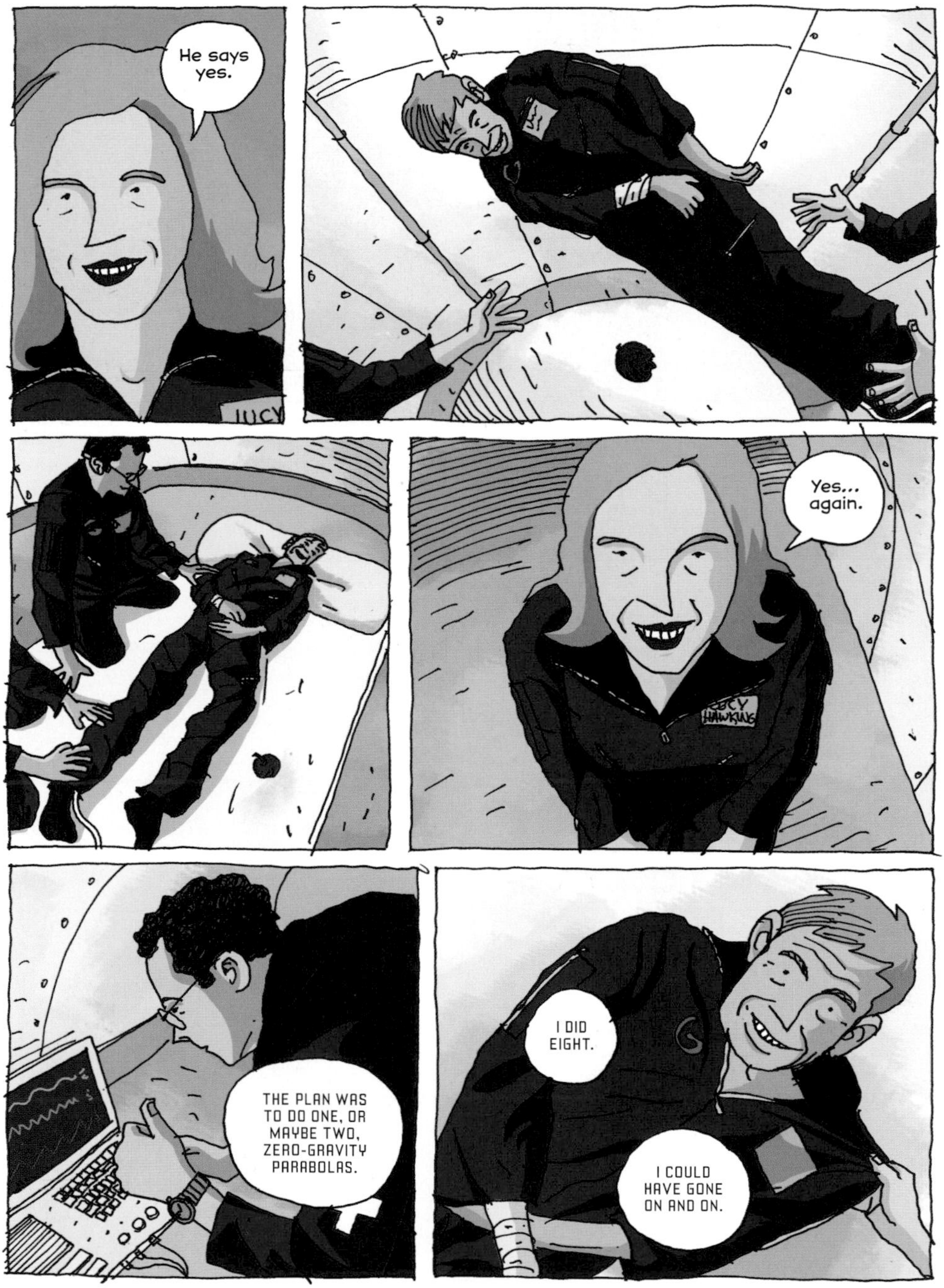

He says yes.
JUCY
Yes... again.
LUCY HAWKING
THE PLAN WAS TO DO ONE, OR MAYBE TWO, ZERO-GRAVITY PARABOLAS.
I DID EIGHT.
I COULD HAVE GONE ON AND ON.

Scientific work (2009–2018)

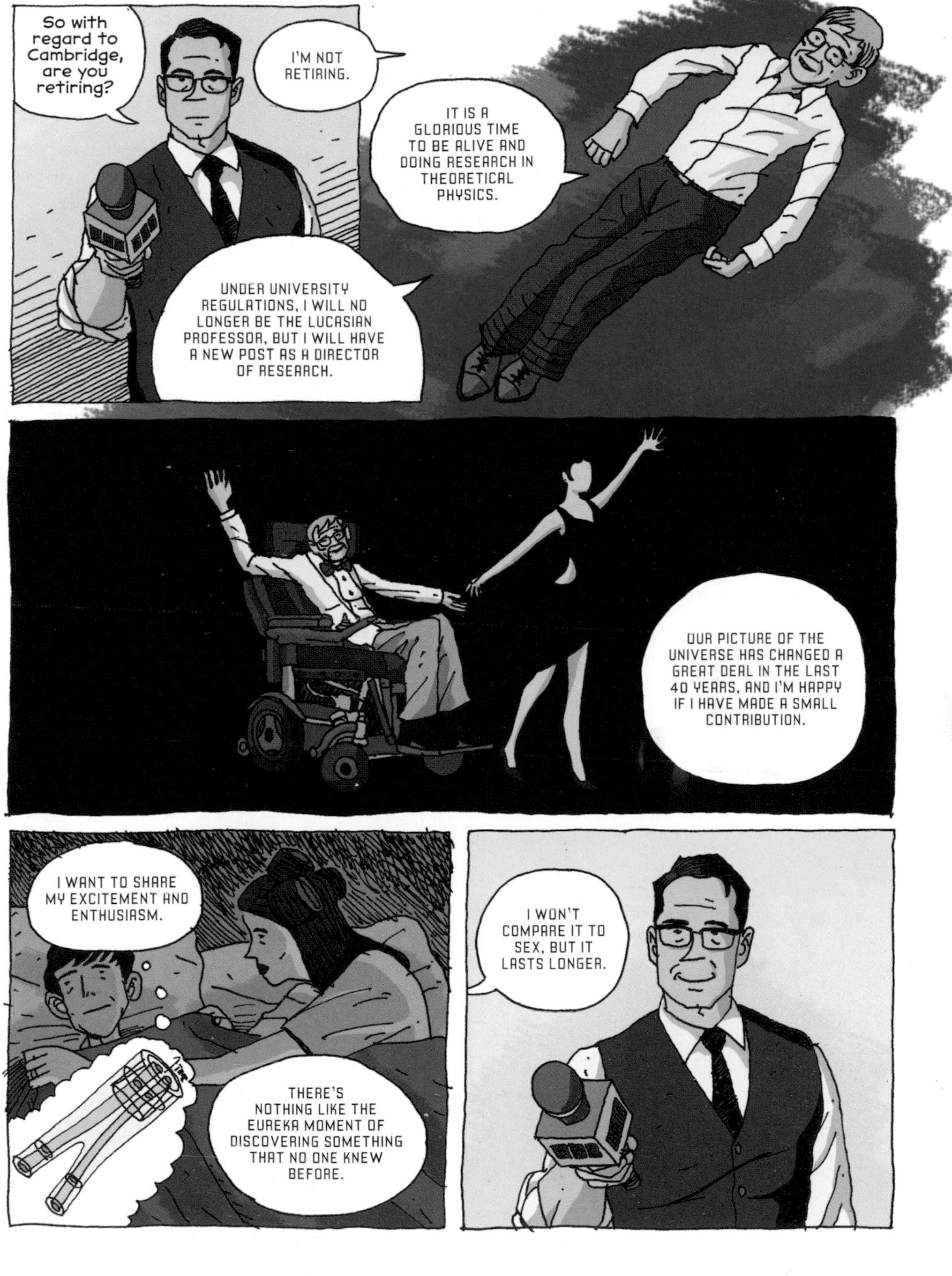
So with regard to Cambridge, are you retiring?
I'M NOT RETIRING.
IT IS A GLORIOUS TIME TO BE ALIVE AND DOING RESEARCH IN THEORETICAL PHYSICS.
UNDER UNIVERSITY REGULATIONS, I WILL NO LONGER BE THE LUCASIAN PROFESSOR, BUT I WILL HAVE A NEW POST AS A DIRECTOR OF RESEARCH.
OUR PICTURE OF THE UNIVERSE HAS CHANGED A GREAT DEAL IN THE LAST 40 YEARS, AND I'M HAPPY IF I HAVE MADE A SMALL CONTRIBUTION.
I WANT TO SHARE MY EXCITEMENT AND ENTHUSIASM.
THERE'S NOTHING LIKE THE EUREKA MOMENT OF DISCOVERING SOMETHING THAT NO ONE KNEW BEFORE.
I WON'T COMPARE IT TO SEX, BUT IT LASTS LONGER.

I WILL CARRY ON WITH MY SCIENTIFIC WORK, AND WITH MY EFFORTS TO EXPLAIN IT TO OTHER PEOPLE.

THOUGH I'M NO LONGER THE LUCASIAN PROFESSOR, I AM STILL A FELLOW AT GONVILLE AND CAIUS COLLEGE.

THAT MEANS I HAVE USE OF THE FACILITIES HERE TO CONDUCT A SIMPLE EXPERIMENT.

ONE THAT COULD REVEAL WHETHER TIME-TRAVEL THROUGH A WORM-HOLE WAS POSSIBLE NOW. OR EVEN IN THE FUTURE.

I LIKE SIMPLE EXPERIMENTS. AND CHAMPAGNE.

SO I THREW A PARTY, A WELCOME RECEPTION FOR FUTURE TIME TRAVELERS.

WELCOME TIME TRAVELLERS

282

BUT I DIDN'T LET ANYONE KNOW ABOUT IT UNTIL AFTER THE PARTY HAD HAPPENED.

NOT EVEN KIP.

THE INVITATION GAVE THE EXACT COORDINATES IN TIME AND SPACE.

IF COPIES OF IT SURVIVE, IN SOME FORM, FOR MANY THOUSANDS OF YEARS, THEN MAYBE SOMEONE WILL USE THEM TO COME BACK TO ATTEND.

You are cordially invited to a reception for Time Travellers,

Hosted by Professor Stephen Hawking

To be held at University of Cambridge Gonville and Caius College Trinity Street Cambridge

Location; 52° 12' 21" N, 0° 7' 4.7"

Time: 12:00 UT 06/28/200

No RSVP required

PROVING THAT TIME TRAVEL IS POSSIBLE.

FIVE... FOUR... THREE... TWO...

ONE...

I WAS HOPING A FUTURE MISS UNIVERSE WAS GOING TO STEP THROUGH.

KIP WOULD NOT HAVE BEEN SURPRISED THAT SHE DIDN'T.

No, not at all.

So yes, I suppose there is a tendency for him to seem oracular.

When Stephen issues a pronouncement, we sometimes can't be sure whether he's just speculating or has strong evidence.

Sometimes he doesn't say. But that smile of his is a tell...

He does, after all, retain a streak of impishness and a sense of humor.

They rarely desert him...

Theory of Everything

I've spoken with your colleagues, and now I'd like to ask you...

You once suggested that you hoped the theory of everything could be found by the end of the century.

ZZNT

Do you think that is a realistic goal?

YES, IN 1980, I SAID THAT A THEORY OF EVERYTHING MIGHT BE FOUND BY THE END OF THE CENTURY.

THAT IS STILL MY ESTIMATE, BUT THERE'S A LOT MORE OF THE CURRENT CENTURY LEFT.

Very good. Now, you said that physics after the theory of everything would be like mountaineering after Everest.

What did you mean?

I WOULD HAVE THOUGHT IT WAS FAIRLY OBVIOUS.

LEGS.

IF WE EVER DO FIND THE COMPLETE THEORY OF THE UNIVERSE, IT WOULD BE A GREAT TRIUMPH OF HUMAN REASON.

BUT IT WOULDN'T LEAVE MUCH FOR US TO DO.

SUCTION.

Lucy, speaking of doing things, you now have a book out with your father. What has that meant for you?

Well, in the past few years our relationship has changed because we've been working together.

And that's been a lot of fun.

I get to see how clear-headed he is, what a huge—*encyclopedic*—amount of knowledge he has inside his mind, and how quick he is in his thought process...

I expect he was always like that, and I didn't...

But over time I think he has probably mellowed as well.

And he probably had to climb out of some black holes too.

He *has* climbed out of some black holes.

But the one thing that *hasn't* changed about him is that he has not slowed down.

At all.

He's just been to Chile and to Easter Island, and now he's back, and soon he's off to the USA and—

WELL, I WANT TO SHARE MY EXCITEMENT AND ENTHUSIASM.

OUR PICTURE OF THE UNIVERSE HAS CHANGED A GREAT DEAL IN THE LAST 40 YEARS, AND I'M HAPPY IF I HAVE MADE A SMALL CONTRIBUTION.

MY GOAL HAS ALWAYS BEEN SIMPLE: TO WORK OUT HOW THE UNIVERSE WORKS. WHY IT EXISTS AT ALL. LUCKILY THERE ARE CLUES EVERYWHERE.

THE MOST IMPORTANT ONES ARE RIGHT ABOVE OUR HEADS.

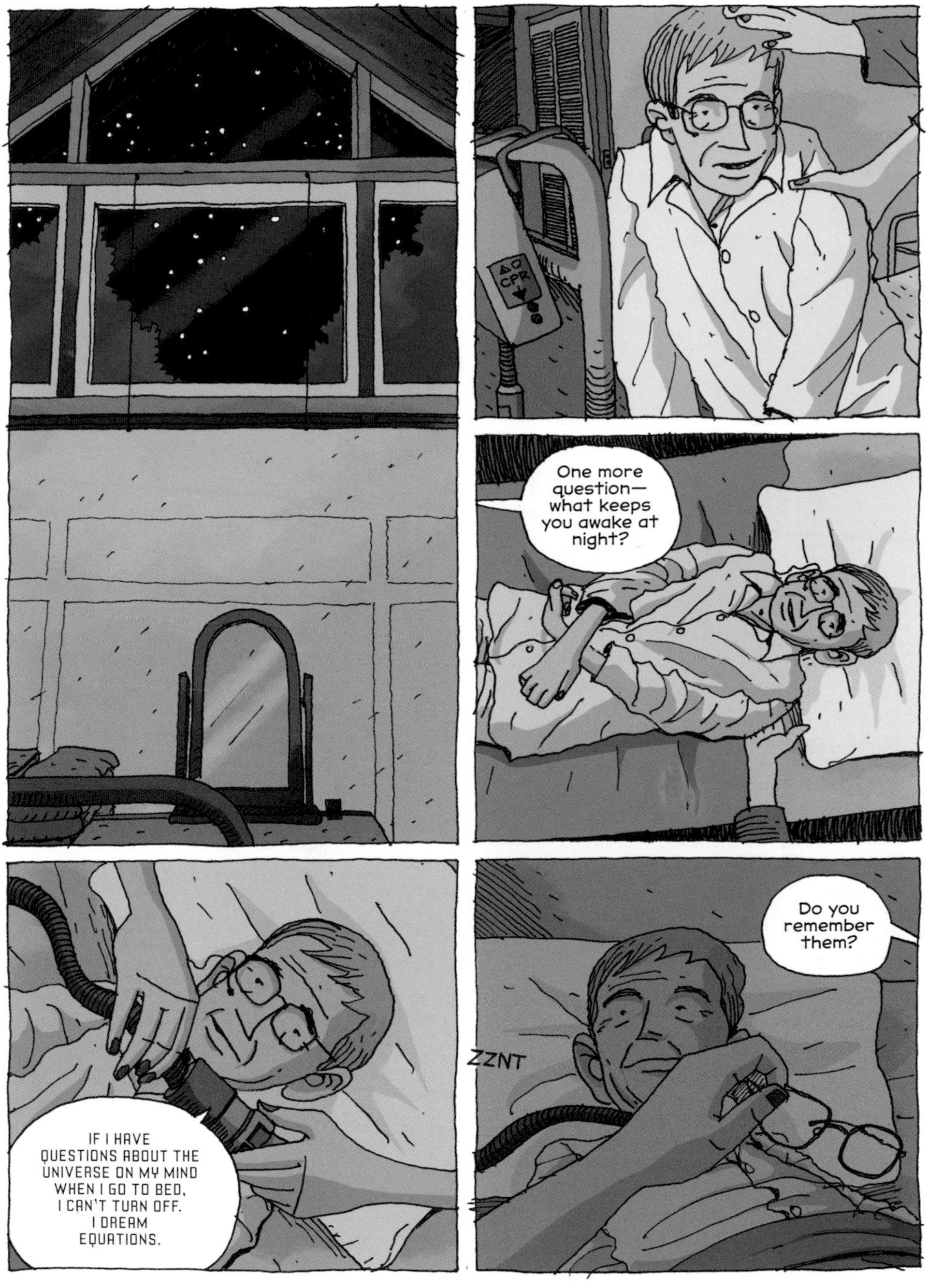

CPR
One more question—what keeps you awake at night?
IF I HAVE QUESTIONS ABOUT THE UNIVERSE ON MY MIND WHEN I GO TO BED, I CAN'T TURN OFF. I DREAM EQUATIONS.
ZZNT
Do you remember them?

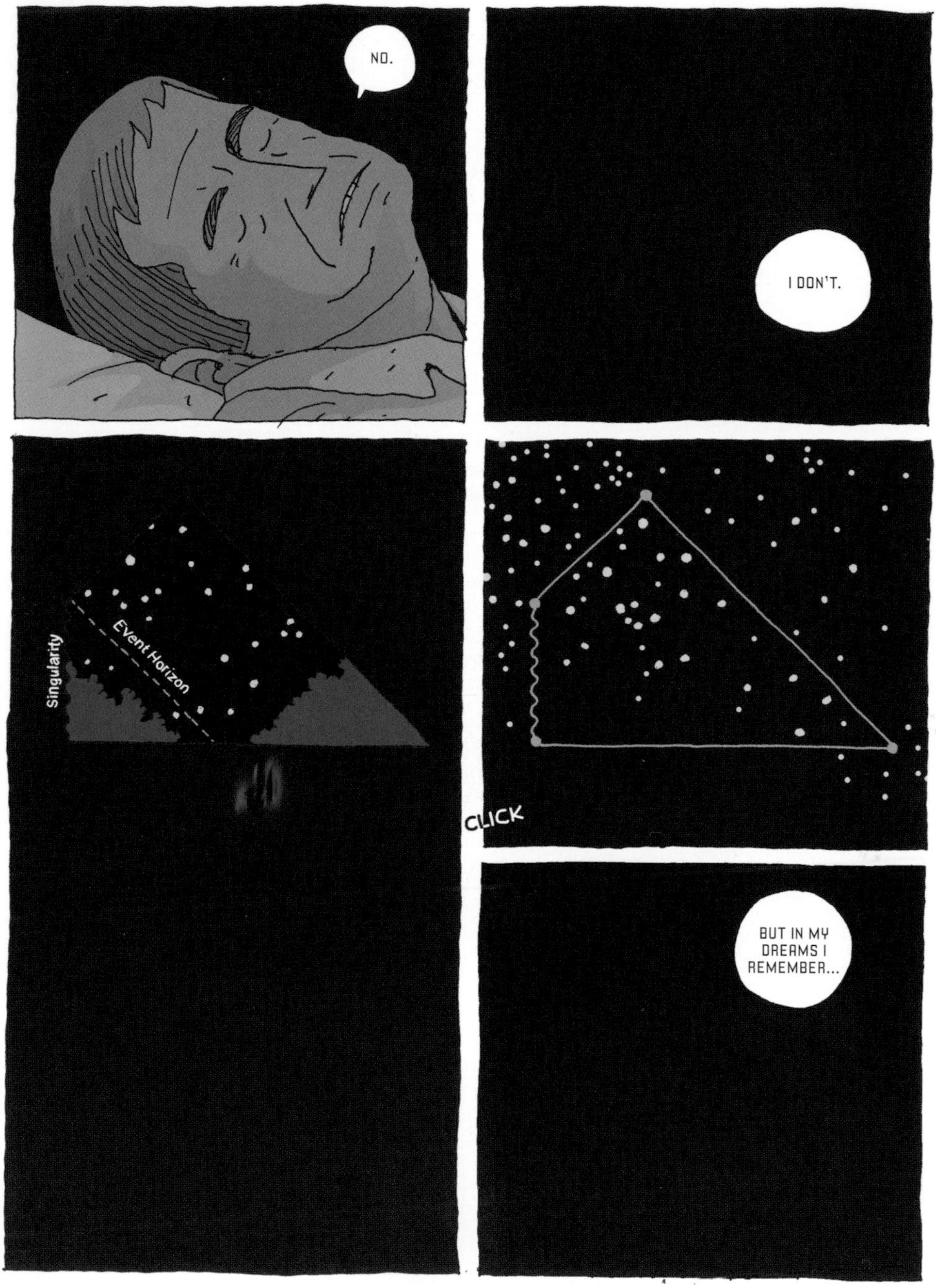
NO.
I DON'T.
Singularity
Event Horizon
CLICK
BUT IN MY DREAMS I REMEMBER...

[redacted]

[redacted]

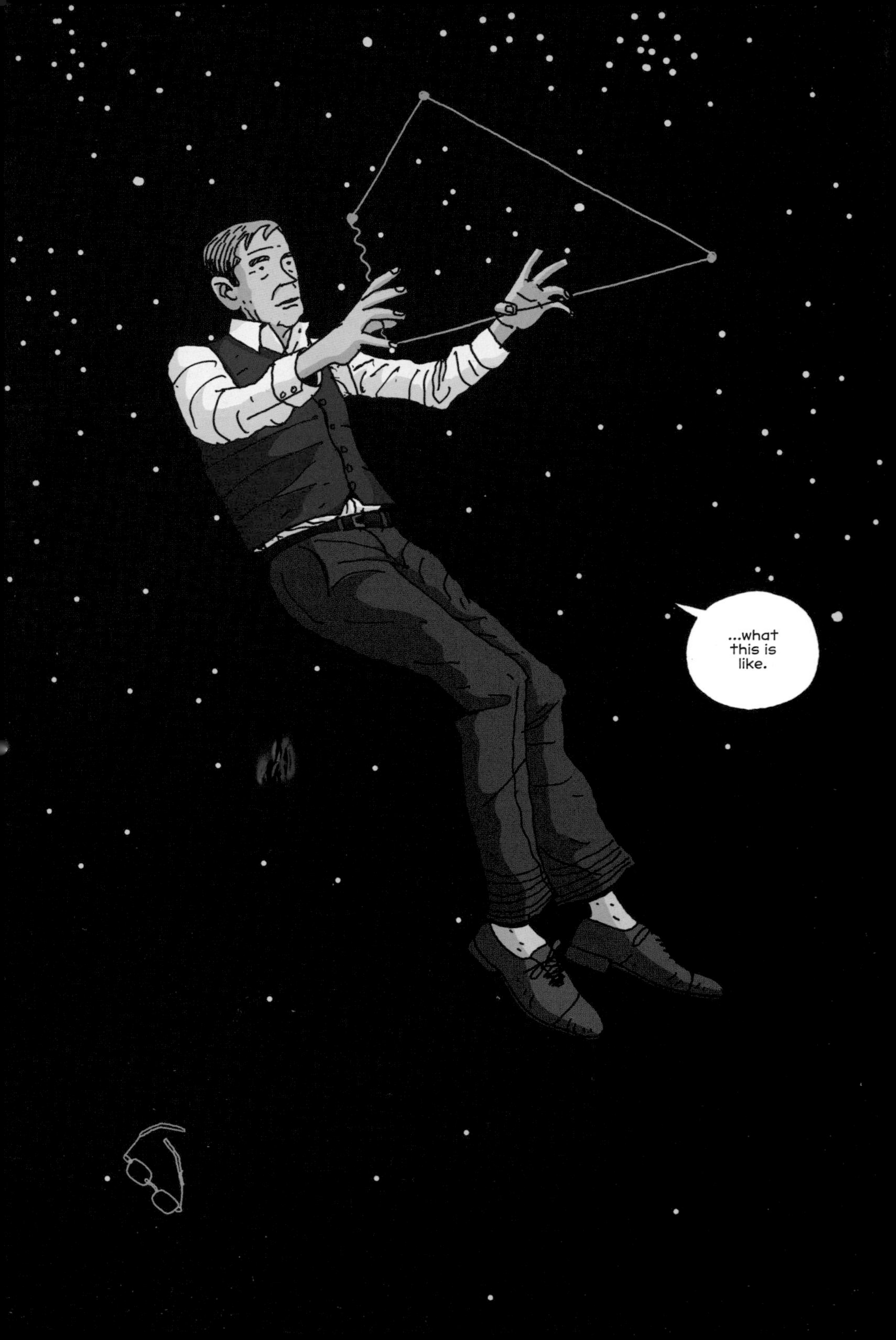
...what this is like.

AUTHOR'S NOTE

Comics is an especially good medium for narrative nonfiction because it integrates words and pictures, leading your mind's eye seamlessly——we hope!——between the two. But even though this is a true story, not all the word balloons and thought bubbles here contain direct quotes. Most of what you read happened as described, and much more often than not the people did and said——or at least wrote—— what you read here. (In case you like numbers, the annotated script for the book that Leland suffered through has more than 400 footnotes sourcing panels and scenes; you can see those sources in the "References" section.) But we did compress certain events and combine characters——Hawking's life touched countless others', after all——and we did imagine some things they might have said in service of constructing what we hope was a satisfying story.

And that story didn't end in the book, so some of the things you read have changed since July 4, 2012, when Hawking——through our friend Lois Kane——invited us to do this. He did write an autobiography (*My Brief History*; see p. 260) and did allow a film of his life (*The Theory of Everything*; mentioned on p. 216). The LIGO experiment detected gravity waves and earned Kip Thorne and his colleagues a Nobel prize (see p. 253). And on that same July day Leland and I knew this was our next book together, Gordy Kane won back his $100 on the Higgs bet (you'll find the terms on p. 236).

Hawking has also passed away, of course, which means having him speak in the present tense also no longer reflects today's reality. But even so, he remains very much alive in our minds, and we hope he's alive in yours as well.

REFERENCES

Books and Videos

Big Bang by Simon Singh (New York: Harper Perennial, 2004).

Beyond the Black Hole by John Boslough (London: Collins, 1985).

Black Holes and Baby Universes and Other Essays by Stephen Hawking (New York: Bantam, 1994).

Black Holes and Warped Spacetime by William J. Kaufmann, III (San Francisco: W.H. Freeman, 1979).

Black Holes and Time Warps by Kip Thorne (New York: Norton, 1994).

Blind Watchers of the Sky by Rocky Kolb (Reading, MA: Addison-Wesley, 1996).

A Brief History of Time by Stephen Hawking (New York: Bantam, 1988).

A [Short/Brief] History of Time manuscript/draft version(s) from the Archive.

A Brief History of Time, producer, Gordon Freeman; director, Errol Morris (Norwich, UK: Anglia Television, 1991).

A Brief History of Time: A Reader's Companion by Stephen Hawking (ed.) and Gene Stone (New York: Bantam, 1992).

A Briefer History of Time by Stephen Hawking and Leonard Mlodinow (New York: Bantam, 2005).

The Cosmic Frontiers of General Relativity by William J. Kaufmann, III (Boston: Little Brown, 1977).

Cosmic Imagery by John Barrow (New York: Norton, 2009).

The Day Without Yesterday by John Farrell (New York: Thunder's Mouth Press, 2005).

The First Three Minutes by Steven Weinberg (New York: Basic Books, 1977).

The Future of Spacetime by Stephen Hawking, Kip S. Thorne, Igor Novikov, Timothy Ferris, Alan Lightman, and Richard Price (New York: Norton, 1992).

The Future of Theoretical Physics and Cosmology: Proceedings of the Stephen Hawking 60th Birthday Conference, edited by G. W. Gibbons, E. P. S. Shellard, S. J. Rankin (New York: Cambridge University Press, 2003).

The Grand Design by Stephen Hawking and Leonard Mlodinow (New York: Bantam, 2010).

Gravity's Engines by Caleb Scharf (New York: Scientific American/Farrar, Straus and Giroux, 2012).

Gravity's Fatal Attraction, 2nd ed., by Mitchell Begelman and Martin Rees (Cambridge: Cambridge University Press, 2010).

Hawking, director and producer, Stephen Finnigan (London: Vertigo Films, 2013).

Hawking Incorporated by Hélène Mialet (Chicago: The University of Chicago Press, 2012).

The Illustrated A Brief History of Time, updated and expanded ed., by Stephen Hawking (New York: Bantam, 1996).

Into the Universe with Stephen Hawking, Gaiam Americas, Inc., Darlow Smithson Productions (Boulder, CO: Gaiam, 2011).

The Large Scale Structure of Space-Time by Stephen Hawking and George Ellis (Cambridge: Cambridge University Press, 1973).

Lonely Hearts of the Cosmos by Dennis Overbye (New York: Harper Collins, 1991).

Memoirs of the Life, Writings, and Discoveries of Sir Isaac Newton (1855) by Sir David Brewster (Volume II. Ch. 27, p. 407).

Music to Move the Stars by Jane Hawking (Tuggerah: Pan Macmillan Australia, 1999).

My Brief History by Stephen Hawking (New York: Bantam, 2013).

The Nature of Space and Time by Stephen Hawking and Roger Penrose (Princeton: Princeton University Press, 1996).

Perfectly Reasonable Deviations from the Beaten Track by Richard Feynman, edited by Michelle Feynman (New York: Basic Books, 2005).

The Primeval Atom: *an Essay on Cosmogony* by G. Lemaître (New York: Van Nostrand, 1950).

Relativity by Albert Einstein (New York: Crown, 1961).

The Road to Reality by Roger Penrose (New York: Knopf, 2006).

Stephen Hawking by Kitty Ferguson (New York: Palgrave Macmillan, 2012).

Stephen Hawking by Melissa McDaniel (New York: Chelsea House, 1994).

Stephen Hawking: A Biography by Kristine Larsen (Westport, CT: Greenwood Press, 2005).

Stephen Hawking: A Life in Science by Michael White and John Gribbin (New York: Dutton, 1992).

Stephen Hawking's Universe: The Cosmos Explained by David Filkin, with a foreword by Stephen Hawking (New York: Basic Books, 1998).

Stephen Hawking's Universe, Uden Associates, David Filkin Enterprises co-production in association with BBC-TV; series producer, David Filkin; series director, Philip Martin (Alexandria, VA: PBS Home Video, 1997).

'Subtle Is the Lord...': The Science and Life of Albert Einstein by Abraham Pais (Oxford: Oxford University Press, 1982).

Traveling to Infinity by Jane Hawking (Richmond: Alma Books, 2007).

The Universe in a Nutshell by Stephen Hawking (New York: Bantam, 2001).

The Universe Within by Neil Turok (Toronto: House of Anansi, 2012).

The Very Early Universe: Proceedings of the Nuffield Workshop, Cambridge, 21 June to 9 July, 1982, edited by G. W. Gibbons and S. W. Hawking and S. T. C. Siklos. (Cambridge: Cambridge University Press, 1983).

Articles

These articles——listed chronologically, in case you want to trace the ideas through (space-) time——will make you look and feel erudite when you read them on the subway; better still, they are readable, at least in large part, even if you don't look at, much less understand, all the equations.

Albert Abraham Michelson and Edward Williams Morley, "On the Relative Motion of the Earth and the Luminiferous Ether," *American Journal of Science*, vol. 34 (1887): 333–345.

Grote Reber, "Cosmic Static," *Astrophysical Journal*, vol. 100 (1944): 279. doi: 10.1086/144668

John Archibald Wheeler, "Our Universe: The Known and the Unknown," *American Scientist* vol. 56, no. 1 (Spring 1968): 34A, 1–20.

S. W. Hawking, "Gravitational Radiation from Colliding Black Holes," *Physical Review Letters* vol. 26 (1971): 1344–1346. http://link.aps.org/doi/10.1103/PhysRevLett.26.1344, doi:10.1103/PhysRevLett.26.1344

Remo Ruffini and John A. Wheeler, "Introducing the Black Hole," *Physics Today* vol. 24, no. 1 (1971): 30–41. doi: http://dx.doi.org/10.1063/1.3022513

S. W. Hawking, "The Event Horizon," in *Black Holes*, ed. C. DeWitt and B. S. DeWitt (New York: Gordon and Breach, 1973), 1–55.

J. M. Bardeen, B. Carter, and S. W. Hawking, "The Four Laws of Black Hole Mechanics," *Communications in Mathematical Physics* vol. 31, no. 2 (1973): 161–170.

S. W. Hawking, "Black Hole Explosions?" *Nature* vol. 248 (1 March 1974): 30–31. doi:10.1038/248030a0

B. Carter, "Large Number Coincidences and the Anthropic Principle in Cosmology" in: *Confrontation of Cosmological Theories with Observational Data*, M. S. Longair, ed. (Dordrecht: Reidel, 1974), 291–298. Reprinted in: *Modern Cosmology & Philosophy*, J. Leslie ed., 2nd ed. (Amherst, New York: Prometheus Books, 1998), 131–139.

S. W. Hawking, "Black Holes and Unpredictability," *Annals of the New York Academy of Sciences*, vol. 302, Eighth Texas Symposium on Relativistic Astrophysics (December 1977): 158–160. doi:10.1111/j.1749-6632.1977.tb37044.x

Ian Ridpath, "Black Hole Explorer," *New Scientist* (4 May 1978): 307–309.

B. J. Carr and M. J. Rees, "The Anthropic Principle and the Structure of the Physical World," *Nature* vol. 278 (12 April 1979): 605–612. doi:10.1038/278605a0

S. W. Hawking, "Arrow of Time in Cosmology," *Physical Review D* vol. 32, no. 10 (1985): 2489–2495. doi:10.1103/PhysRevD.32.2489

S. W. Hawking, "Inflation Reputation Reparation," *Physics Today* (February 1989): 15, 123.

S. W. Hawking, "Chronology Protection Conjecture," *Physical Review D* vol. 46 (1992): 603–611. doi:10.1103/PhysRevD.46.603

S. W. Hawking, "Information Loss in Black Holes," *Physical Review D* vol. 72 (2005): 084013. doi:10.1103/PhysRevD.72.084013

C. Montgomery, W. Orchiston, and I. Whittingham, "Michell, Laplace and the Origin of the Black Hole Concept," *Journal of Astronomical History and Heritage* vol. 12, no. 2 (2009): 90–96. http://articles.adsabs.harvard.edu/full/2009JAHH...12...90M

People

Special thanks to friends Lois and Gordy Kane, Malcolm Perry and Anna Zytkow, Stephen Hawking's personal assistant Judith Croasdell, and Yvonne Nobis of the Betty & Gordon Moore Library. They gave us the gifts of their encouragement, kindness, and time . . . not to mention access to ideas and people and places and things beyond what we could have dreamed of on our own. And even though our visit didn't go 100% to plan, having Stephen Hawking invite you to come to Cambridge and discuss making a comic book about him is as fantastic as you think it is. The day Lois relayed his invitation made it not just a big day for people who bet on the Higgs boson, but for us as well. We're grateful.

From that day until now even more people helped us get this book done, and make it look good, so cheers to Andrew, Angelo, Anne, Bobby, Calista, Casey, Christine, Jerzy, Kayla, Kiara, Mark, Molly, Rob, Robyn, and Tara.

JIM OTTAVIANI is a *New York Times*–bestselling author who began writing graphic novels about scientists in 1997. His most recent books are *Astronauts* (a biography about Mary Cleave, Valentina Tereshkova, Sally Ride, and the first women in space), *The Imitation Game* (a biography of Alan Turing), *Primates* (a biography about Jane Goodall, Dian Fossey, and Biruté Galdikas), and *Feynman* (a biography about the Nobel Prize–winning physicist, bongo-playing artist, and raconteur Richard Feynman).

LELAND MYRICK is the Ignatz Award– and Harvey Award– nominated author and illustrator of *The Sweet Collection*, *Bright Elegy*, and *Missouri Boy* and the illustrator of the #1 *New York Times* bestseller *Feynman*. He has written and illustrated work for Dark Horse Comics, *GQ Japan*, *Vogue Russia*, and the Flight series.